Gwell Angau Na Chywilydd

Death Rather Than Dishonour

A
Concise History
of
The Royal Welsh
(23rd, 24th, 41st and 69th Foot)

COLONEL-IN-CHIEF
HER MAJESTY THE QUEEN

Gwell Angau Na Chywilydd (Death Rather Than Dishonour)
A Concise History of The Royal Welsh (23rd, 24th, 41st and 69th Foot)

First published in Wales in 2011 by
BRIDGE BOOKS
61 Park Avenue
WREXHAM
LL12 7AW
on behalf of the
Regimental Committee of
The Royal Welsh

Regimental Headquarters
Maindy Barracks, Cardiff, CF14 3YE
(Telephone: 029 2078 1202 Fax: 029 2078 1357)

North Wales Office
Hightown Barracks, Wrexham, North Wales LL13 8RD
(Telephone: 01978 316187/9 Fax: 01978 316121)

ISBN: 978-1-84494-077-6
A CIP entry for this book is available from the British Library

Printed and bound by
Gutenberg Press Ltd
Malta

CONTENTS

		Page
	Foreword by the Colonel of the Regiment	5
1	Battle Honours of The Royal Welsh	7
2	Lineage of The Royal Welsh since 1689	9
3	A Legacy of Loyal Service	10
4	The 23rd, The Royal Welch Fusiliers	13
5	The 24th, The South Wales Borderers	31
6	The 41st, (The Welsh) Regiment of Foot	39
7	The 69th (South Lincolnshire) Regiment	42
8	The Welch Regiment	44
9	The Royal Regiment of Wales (24th/41st Foot)	49
10	Auxiliary, Reserve and Cadet Forces	52
11	The New Regiment – The Royal Welsh	60
12	Badges, Dress and Distinctions	63
	Badges	63
	Dress	68
	Distinctions	73
13	Customs, Regimental Days, Music and Privileges	77
	Customs	77
	Regimental Days	77
	Regimental Music	79
	Civic Freedoms	80
	Regimental Collect	82
	Allied Regiments	82
	Bonds of Friendship	83
	What's in a Name	83
14	The Regimental Association	86
15	A Selection of Published Regimental Histories	88

16 Sporting Achievements 94
17 Regimental Museums and Chapels 99
18 The Literary Tradition 102

Appendices
A Recipients of The Victoria Cross and The George Cross 105
B Colonels of the Regiment 108
C Lieutenant Colonels Commanding 113
D Chronology of Regimental Events since 1689 114

Note on the spelling of regimental titles

The spelling of Welsh or Welch used in the titles of the former regiments in this publication might cause confusion, or even to some readers, dismay. There is a full explanation in Section 13,'What's in a Name'. Generally, the official army spelling 'Welsh' was in use prior to 1920, although the regiments themselves tended to adhere to the much older spelling 'Welch'. This anomaly was finally resolved in January 1920 when official approval to use the more traditional spelling 'Welch' was finally conferred on the antecedent regiments of The Royal Welsh by the Army Board.

Preface to *The Uncommercial Traveller* (1861)

Any animated description of a modern battle, any private soldier's letter published in the newspapers, any page of the records of the Victoria Cross, will show that in the ranks of the Army there exists under all disadvantages as fine a sense of duty as to be found in any station on earth. Who doubts that if we did our duty as faithfully as the soldier does his, this world would be a better place? There may be greater difficulties in our way than in the soldier's. Not disputed. But let us at least do our duty toward him.

Charles Dickens

FOREWORD

by

Major-General RJM Porter MBE
Colonel of the Regiment
The Royal Welsh
(2006–11)

The Royal Welsh is now the only line infantry regiment of Wales and has inherited a distinguished military tradition from its predecessors, The Royal Welch Fusiliers and The Royal Regiment of Wales. Although, in some respects, our story only began on 1st March 2006, we are actually the inheritors of a legacy that reaches back to 1689. Our story is a continuation of that of our forebears and we are proud to pick up and carry forward the torch that they bore in their time. It is therefore a great honour for me, as the first Colonel of The Royal Welsh, to be asked to write the Foreword to this short recounting of that history.

The events of St David's Day 2006, our Formation Day, proved to be a fitting tribute to our founding Regiments. A Drumhead Service, with the Colours on parade, dedicating The Royal Welsh for service before God and the people of Wales, was also an opportunity to remember those who had made the ultimate sacrifice and to appreciate our rich and diverse military heritage.

I believe it is important that we should preserve all the customs and traditions of our antecedent regiments. That is why I have commissioned this short history which brings together, for the first time in one document, the major events that form the bedrock of our regiment's heritage. I have no doubt that, over time, unique Royal Welsh traditions will emerge and older ones will be adapted; history will continue to be written and valour is still displayed on the field of battle. The history of great regiments does not disappear with a cherished cap badge; it is revered and retold and provides inspiration to new generations of soldiers.

Our antecedents often fought side-by-side in the great and bloody struggles that have marked our nation's contribution to world events; such was the case in no fewer than 63 battles of the Great War (1914–18). This is not surprising as our regiments made up the greater part of the famous Welsh Divisions – the

38th and 53rd. From the Second World War, there are fifteen shared battle honours, mostly from North West Europe where the 53rd (Welsh) Division fought from Normandy to Hamburg between June 1944 and May 1945. In more recent times they have served in Northern Ireland, Germany, Bosnia and the Falkland Islands. Now, five years beyond the merger, both the regiment's Regular battalions, ably supported by our Territorial Battalion, have already distinguished themselves time and again on operations in Iraq and Afghanistan. Our common bond has often been cemented in the cross-posting of officers and soldiers between Welsh infantry regiments. This now continues between battalions of The Royal Welsh, providing greater career opportunities and operational experience for all.

I am delighted that Her Majesty The Queen agreed in 2006 to become our Colonel-in-Chief. This is a signal honour and we have already had the privilege of formally welcoming her to the regiment on two occasions:; the first at Tidworth to celebrate our first anniversary on Saint David's Day 2007; the second at Chester Racecourse in June 2010 to welcome the 1st Battalion home from Afghanistan. We look forward to many further such visits to the regiment in the future. We also anticipate keenly the challenges and opportunities that lie ahead. Each period of history is unique and The Royal Welsh is proud to have been given the opportunity, in our generation, to add to the illustrious pages of history that constitute our heritage; opportunity already seized magnificently on Operations HERRICK and TELIC.

Finally, I am very grateful to Martin Everett, ably assisted by Richard Sinnett, for their dedicated hard work in producing this narrative which I am sure will be of great interest to serving members of the regiment, to our many supporters worldwide and, most importantly, to those about to embark on a career with the regiment.

Gwell Angau Na Chywilydd

Section 1

BATTLE HONOURS OF THE ROYAL WELSH
(23RD, 24TH, 41ST AND 69TH)

The Cap Badge – the badge of Heir Apparent with a scroll below inscribed THE ROYAL WELSH

The Queen's Colour – a Silver Wreath of Immortelles borne around the colour pikeborne around the colour pike. The Union Colour with the badge of the Heir Apparent within a circlet inscribed THE ROYAL WELSH surmounted by The Crown, together with the 43 selected Honours (those in bold below) from the Great War and Second World War.

The Regimental Colour – the badge of the Heir Apparent within a circlet inscribed THE ROYAL WELSH within the Union Wreath surmounted by the Crown, across the tie of the Wreath a scroll inscribed with the motto GWELL ANGAU NA CHYWILYDD; the Battle Honours of the regiment with a Naval Crown superscribed 12TH APRIL 1782 subscribed ST VINCENT 1797. In the first quarter The Royal Cypher. In the second quarter the Red Dragon Rampant. In third quarter the White Horse of Hanover with motto NEC ASPERA TERRENT. In the fourth quarter the Rising Sun. The Sphinx superscribed EGYPT above a laurel wreath at the base.

The Honours for Egypt (1801), The Saints (12th April 1782) and St Vincent (1797) do not have separate scrolls as they are incorporated as part of the distinctive badges emblazoned on the Regimental Colour. Those 46 selected Honours dating from before the Great War (those in bold below) and Korea 1951–52 are emblazoned on the Regimental Colour:

Namur 1695 + **Blenheim** + **Ramillies** + **Oudenarde** + **Malplaquet** + **Dettingen** + **Minden** + **Belleisle** + **Martinique 1762, 1809** + **India** + **Cape of Good Hope 1806** + **Corunna** + **Talavera** + **Bourbon** + **Busaco** + **Fuentes d'Onor** + **Albuhera** + **Java** + **Badajoz** + **Salamanca** + **Detroit** + **Queenstown** + **Miami** + **Vittoria** + **Pyrenees** + **Nivelle** + **Orthes** + **Toulouse** + **Niagara** + Peninsula + **Waterloo** + **Ava** + **Candahar 1842** + **Ghuznee 1842** + **Cabool 1842** + **Chillianwallah** + **Goojerat** + Punjaub + **Alma** + **Inkerman** + **Sevastopol** + **Lucknow** + **Ashantee 1873–4** + **South Africa 1877–8–9** + **Burma 1885–87** + Relief of Kimberley + Paardeberg + Relief of Ladysmith + **South Africa 1899–1902** + **Pekin 1900**.

The Great War – **Mons** + Le Cateau + Retreat from Mons + **Marne 1914** + **Aisne 1914, 18** + La Bassée 1914 + Messines 1914, 17, 18 + Armentières 1914 + **Ypres 1914, 15, 17, 18** + Langemarck 1914, 17 + **Gheluvelt** + Nonne Bosschen + Givenchy 1914 + Neuve Chapelle + Gravenstafel + St Julien + Frezenberg + Bellewaarde + Aubers + Festubert 1915 + **Loos** + **Somme 1916, 18** + Albert 1916, 18 + Bazentin + Delville Wood + Pozières + Guillemont + Flers-Courcelette + Morval + Le Transloy + Ancre Heights + Ancre 1916, 18 + Arras 1917, 18 + Scarpe 1917 + Arleux + Bullecourt + **Pilckem** + Menin Road + Polygon Wood + Broodseinde + Poelcappelle + Passchendaele + **Cambrai 1917, 18** + St Quentin + Bapaume 1918 + Lys + Estaires + Hazebrouck + Bailleul + Kemmel + Béthune + Scherpenberg + Drocourt-Quéant + **Hindenburg Line** + Havrincourt + Épéhy + St Quentin Canal + Beaurevoir + Courtrai + Selle + Valenciennes + Sambre + France and Flanders 1914–18 + Piave + **Vittorio Veneto** + Italy 1917–18 + Struma + **Doiran 1917, 18** + Macedonia 1915–18 + Helles + **Landing at Helles** + Krithia + Suvla + Sari Bair + Landing at Suvla + Scimitar Hill + **Gallipoli 1915–16** + Rumani + **Egypt 1915–17** + **Gaza** + El Mughar + Jerusalem + Jericho + Tell 'Asur + Megiddo + Nablus + Palestine 1917–18 + Aden + Tigris 1916 + Kut al Amara 1917 + **Baghdad** + Mesopotamia 1916–18 + **Tsingtao**.

The Second World War – **Norway 1940** + Dyle + Defence of Escaut + **St Omer–La Bassée** + **Normandy Landing** + **Sully** + Odon + **Caen** + Esquay + Bourguebus Ridge + Mont Pinçon + Souleuvre + Le Perier Ridge + **Falaise** + Risle Crossing + Antwerp + **Le Havre** + Nederrijn + Antwerp–Turnhout Canal + Scheldt + **Lower Maas** + Venlo Pocket + Zetten + Ourthe + Rhineland + **Reichswald** + Goch + **Weeze** + Hochwald + **Rhine** + Ibbenbüren + Aller + Arnhem 1945 + North-West Europe 1940, 44–45 + Benghazi + Gazala + **North Africa 1940–42** + Sicily 1943 + Coriano + **Croce** + Rimini Line + Ceriano Ridge + Argenta Gap + **Italy 1943–45** + **Crete** + **Canea** + Withdrawal to Sphakia + **Madagascar** + Middle East 1941–42 + **Donbaik** + **North Arakan** + **Mayu Tunnels** + **Kohima** + **Pinwe** + **Kyaukmyaung Bridgehead** + Shweli + Mandalay + Myitson + Ava + Maymyo + Rangoon Road + **Sittang 1945** + **Burma 1943–45**.

Korea 1951–52

Section 2

THE LINEAGE OF THE ROYAL WELSH SINCE 1689

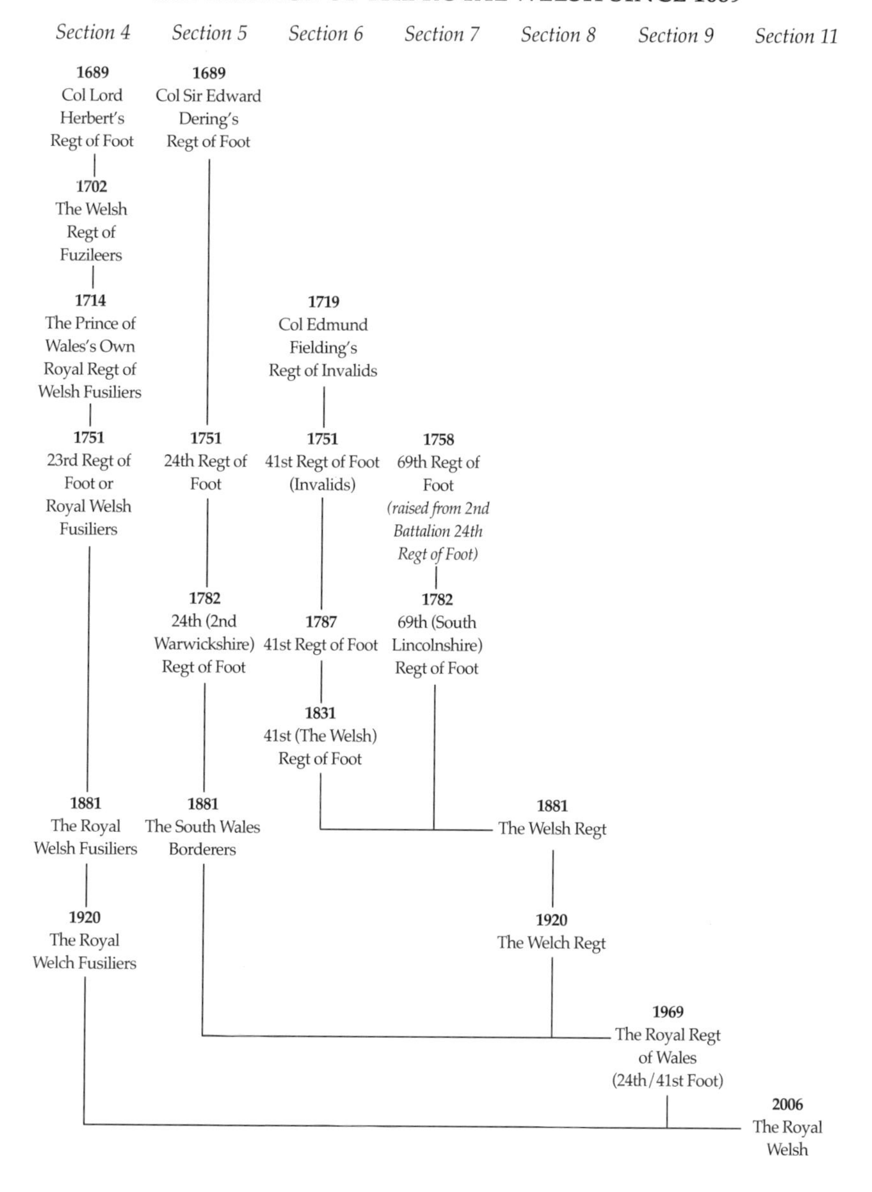

Section 3

A LEGACY OF LOYAL SERVICE

A regiment is much about people and their character; character that has been honed by training, fear, loyalty and bravery, fashioned and hardened by war.

Saint David's Day 2006 saw the formation of a new regiment in the British Army, called 'The Royal Welsh'. This change of structure in the infantry for Wales united the regular and cadet battalions of The Royal Welch Fusiliers and The Royal Regiment of Wales (24th/41st Foot) and the territorials of The Royal Welsh Regiment. The occasion was marked by a ceremonial march-past of the City Hall in Cardiff, where the Right Honourable The Lord Mayor, Councillor Freda Salway, with the Regiment's new Colonel, Brigadier RJM Porter MBE, took the salute. In all, 900 Regular and Territorial Army soldiers, cadets and comrades paraded with their Colours, Branch Standards, the regimental goats, the pioneers, bands and drums. A forecast of poor cold weather meant that the focal point of the day, a Regimental Muster around a Drumhead Service, was held indoors in St David's Hall, rather than the more public Roald Dahl Plâs as planned. This poignant service was conducted by the Army's Chaplain-General assisted by the Brigade and Battalion Chaplains. The service was an opportunity to give thanks, before Almighty God and the people of Wales, for the antecedent regiments; for their traditions, their ethos and the men who have served so faithfully down the years. It was also a chance to remember and honour the sacrifices they had made in times of conflict to ensure peace.

The antecedent regiments have a history and heritage that goes back over 300 years. They were first mustered within days of each other in March 1689, when King William III, in a single commission parchment, charged Lord Herbert of Chirbury and Sir Edward Dering to each raise a regiment of foot for service in Ireland. Since those early days, these regiments have participated in many of the significant events in British history.

Over the years, these regiments' titles have evolved to meet changing roles and national needs. The significant contribution by its soldiers in the two World Wars will alone ensure the names of the 23rd or The Royal Welch Fusiliers, 24th or The South Wales Borderers, and 41st or The Welch Regiment will live in the hearts and memories of many people, particularly those in Wales, for a very long time. The last of the territorial battalions of the Monmouthshire Regiment, inextricably part of the Corps of the South Wales Borderers, disappeared in 1967. For the Great War, the collective figures for these four infantry regiments appear incomprehensible today with 250,000 men serving in 105 battalions, gaining 106 Battle Honours, at a cost of 25,886 lives with many more soldiers maimed and disabled for life. In 1969, tinged with much sadness, the South Wales Borderers and the Welch Regiment amalgamated to form The Royal Regiment of Wales.

The joining together of The Royal Welch Fusiliers and The Royal Regiment of Wales, two distinguished regiments of the line, each with its own distinctive characteristics, has created a regiment which is rich in the traditions of both the old regiments, bonded by their Welsh backgrounds, but a regiment which will immediately develop its own distinctive style and customs.

A glance at The Royal Welsh's history underlines the richness of the fighting heritage of the regiment. There are numerous instances where the antecedent regiments found themselves fighting side by side, in Marlborough's campaigns, in the Crimea, at Mametz Wood in the Great War and in bringing freedom to the Dutch city of 's-Hertogenbosch in 1944. Throughout time, individual officers and soldiers have been inter-posted between regiments contributing to a strong blend of mutual comradeship and understanding.

The Royal Welch Fusiliers distinguished itself in many campaigns; of note are Minden in 1759, Yorktown in America, Albuhera in the Peninsula, the seizing of the Great Redoubt at the Alma in the Crimea, the Relief of Lucknow during the Mutiny in India, the unique Honour gained after the Boxer rebellion in Peking and their heroic stand in 1944 at Kohima on the borders of India.

The South Wales Borderers, who are closely associated with Brecon and its cathedral, are perhaps best remembered for Marlborough's campaigns when the Duke was their Colonel, the American War of Independence, in the Peninsula at Talavera and in the Sikh wars at Chillianwallah. Its involvement in the Zulu campaign was both tragic and glorious; Isandlwana and Rorke's

Drift are likely to be remembered for a long time.

The Welch Regiment, formed in 1719 as a Regiment of Invalids for garrison duties, went on to distinguish itself in a wide variety of campaigns, most notably in Canada, the Napoleonic wars (in which elements served at both Waterloo and with the Royal Navy as naval infantry), in the Crimea, not to mention the two World Wars and afterwards in Korea.

In more recent times, soldiers of the Royal Welch Fusiliers and the Royal Regiment of Wales have played a vital role during operational tours in Northern Ireland, the Balkans and in Iraq, gaining many honours, individual awards and much praise for their steadfastness and professionalism, combined with their typical Welsh humour and sense of fair play. These attributes were soon tested after formation, when both regular battalions, together with a number of Territorial soldiers from the 3rd Battalion, were deployed to Afghanistan and Iraq in 2007.

The regiment has gained 244 Battle Honours, far more that can be displayed on the Colours, and 43 of its soldiers have received Britain's highest award for valour – The Victoria Cross (for a list of recipients see Appendix A). But above all else, the regiment has today a strong sense of identity with Wales and its people, which gives all its battalions (regular, reserve and cadet) a distinct flair and *ésprit de corps*. It is predicted that The Royal Welsh will emulate the fine standards and traditions of its gallant forebears, to make it one of the finest regiments in the British Army.

This booklet can only give an introduction to The Royal Welsh's rich history. The evolution of antecedent regiments, in particular the volunteer and reserve battalions, is too complex to be covered in any depth here. For those who desire greater detail, there exist some very comprehensive and readable regimental histories (see Section 16). The regiment's three fine museums can also help in this regard and are well worth a visit (see Section 18).

Section 4

23RD THE ROYAL WELCH FUSILIERS

23RD REGIMENT OF FOOT
1689–1751

Early Days – Lord Herbert's Regiment
The overthrow of James II and the succession of William III and Mary in early 1689 signalled a major expansion of the Army to oppose James's French and Irish troops in Ireland and the imminent war with France. On 16th March 1689, Henry, 4th Lord Herbert of Chirbury, received a warrant to raise volunteers for a regiment to be assembled at Ludlow, with precedence soon to be granted as the 23rd Regiment of Foot. In the following month he handed over to his cousin Charles, and by August Lord Herbert's Regiment joined the army in Ireland to deal with the threat posed by James and his French allies. In June 1690, King William joined his troops in Ireland and on the 1st July led them to victory at the battle of the Boyne. The regiment remained in Ireland and in 1691 took part in the victory at Aughrim, where their Colonel, Charles Herbert, was 'unfortunately taken prisoner, and a few hours later barbarously murdered to prevent his being rescued'.

War of the Spanish Succession
In 1694, the regiment landed on continental Europe and in the following year participated in the siege of Namur, where it earned its first Battle Honour. In 1701, after a short period in England and Ireland, war broke out, and the regiment was ordered to Holland where it was placed under the command of John Churchill, shortly to become the Duke of Marlborough. The regiment fought in all Marlborough's major battles – Blenheim, Ramillies, Oudenarde and Malplaquet – and remained in Holland until after peace had been signed at Utrecht in 1713.

Until 1702, the regiment, in common with most others, was known by the name of its Colonel, but as a newspaper of the time reported, 'Major General Ingoldsby's [the Colonel] Regiment is to be formed into a regiment of Fusiliers, and will be called the Welsh Regiment of Fuzileers'. The specific task of fusilier regiments was to protect the artillery. This was because they were armed with the early flintlock, known as the fusil, a much safer weapon to use when near gunpowder. When the flintlock was issued to all the infantry in the early eighteenth-century the Fusiliers lost their special role, but the three regiments, 7th, 21st and 23rd, succeeded in establishing themselves as élite regiments. In 1713, as a reward for its great gallantry under Marlborough, the regiment was styled 'The Royal Regiment of Welsh Fuzileers' and the following year, as a result of its close connection with the Prince of Wales, it was authorised to bear on the Colours three of his badges: The Red Dragon, The Rising Sun and the Crest of The Prince of Wales.

War of the Austrian Succession

For the next 30 years the regiment remained in England, with occasional forays north of the border, once to help in the suppression of the Porteous Riots in Edinburgh. Peace, which rarely lasted for long in eighteenth-century Europe, ended in 1740 although Britain managed to avoid involvement until 1742 when an expeditionary force, including the 23rd Foot, sailed for Holland. At the battle of Dettingen in 1743, in which George II was the last British Sovereign to lead his army in battle, Colonel Newsham Peers became the last Colonel of the Welch Fusiliers to lead his regiment in person and died so doing. To commemorate this battle the White Horse of Hanover is carried on the regimental colour. At Fontenoy in 1745, although defeated, the British army was not disgraced, and the 23rd were one of heaviest sufferers, sustaining over 300 casualties. After the battle, as a reward for his gallant conduct, Sergeant Peter Hewitt was granted a commission in the regiment, almost certainly the first recorded incidence in the history of the regiment.

23RD REGIMENT OR ROYAL WELSH FUSILIERS
1751–1881

Seven Years' War

The outbreak of war in 1756 found the 23rd serving as part of the garrison of the island of Minorca, that included the 24th Foot. Britain was on the side of Prussia against Austria, France and Russia. A large French force attacked the island, but the defenders held out for two months. Eventually, the small garrison was overwhelmed and had to surrender. As a mark of respect for their gallant defence, the regiments were allowed to march out with all the honours of war, namely 'fire-locks on their shoulders, drums beating, colours flying ...'. The losses of the Royal Welsh Fusiliers exceeded those of any other regiment.

In the same year, a second battalion of the Royal Welsh Fusiliers was raised, in which Captain Peter Hewitt of Fontenoy fame, was a company commander. In 1758 it was formed into a separate regiment, the 68th, later the Durham Light Infantry.

In July 1759, the 23rd were part of an allied army, under Prince Ferdinand of Brunswick, confronting the French who were established close to the fortress of Minden on the river Weser. Although outnumbered, Ferdinand was determined to bring the French to battle. At last he succeeded and on 1st August the two armies faced each other in battle array. The Royal Welsh Fusiliers were in Waldegrave's Brigade, with the 12th and 37th Regiments, with the 20th, 25th, and 51st forming a second line to the rear. An *aide-de-camp* gave Waldegrave the warning order that 'when the troops advance, they will do so with drums beating'. Waldegrave, assuming this to be an executive order, led his three battalions towards the French cavalry. The latter, with massive artillery support, advanced to the charge. The steadfast British line held its fire until the last, with devastating effect, and dead men and horses soon lay around them. After three hours of fighting, the French army was in flight. The 23rd had suffered forty per cent casualties. The behaviour of the six British battalions was a marvellous example of skill, courage, discipline and firepower. The French commander, Marshal Contades, said later 'I never thought to see a single line of infantry break through three lines of cavalry ranked in order of battle and tumble them to ruin'. The war continued until a peace treaty was signed at Fontainebleau in 1762.

Thirteen years of peace followed which the 23rd spent at home. Following a review by George III in 1771 a newspaper, the *Gazeteer*, reported that 'The Royal Regiment of Welch Fuzileers is as well known to all veterans in Europe as any regiment in their respective nations'.

American War of Independence

In 1773 the regiment sailed for America, where it was soon embroiled in the conflict with the disaffected colonists. The 23rd were in the thick of the fighting and particularly distinguished themselves at the battles of Bunker Hill in 1775 and Guilford Court House in 1781. Leadership of the army in America was less than impressive, and in September 1781 American troops invested Yorktown, the garrison of which included the Royal Welsh Fusiliers. They were holding a redoubt at the end of the line and beat off three major assaults. In the face of overwhelming odds, General Cornwallis offered to surrender. Those who could stand marched out with the Honours of War, and the Colours of the regiment were saved by being concealed under the jackets of officers. The Fusilier Redoubt, with its memorial to the regiment, marks the spot to this day. A contemporary diary records that 'Even the French ... gave the Royal Welsh Fuziliers their unqualified approbation and praise for their intrepidity and firmness in repulsing three attacks made by such vastly superior numbers on the redoubt and could not easily believe that so few men had defended it'. In 1783, the war ended and in the following year the regiment was back in Britain.

French Revolutionary War

The outbreak of the French Revolution in 1789, and the subsequent rise to power of Napoleon, led to almost 25 years of war in Europe and the New World. During the early years, Britain's share of the fighting was limited to naval actions and small expeditions such as those to Santa Domingo (Haiti) in the West Indies, Ostend, North Holland and Ferrol in Spain, in all of which the Royal Welsh Fusiliers took part. In 1797, a number of naval mutinies broke out and the regiment was despatched to the Nore to stop the mutineers from coming ashore. On arrival, an attempt was made to suborn the soldiers, but they resisted and submitted the following address to the King: 'How much we detest the infamous attempts made on the minds of the army of late, in the distribution of certain seditious handbills. We are happy to say that no atrocious villain has ever yet been daring enough to attempt by artifice (or otherwise) to seduce the Royal Welsh Fuzileers from their hitherto unerring fidelity'. It is believed that the King's gratification was such that he gave permission for the officers of the regiment to dispense with the drinking of the Loyal Toast, a tradition which continues to this day.

In 1799, an amphibious expedition was despatched to the Helder to capture the Dutch fleet and raise a rebellion in Holland. The Royal Welsh Fusiliers were amongst the first ashore and secured a beachhead. After the capture of a number of Dutch ships, it was decided to evacuate the force. Nearly half of the regiment, including a number of women and children, were embarked on a captured Dutch frigate, the *Valk*, with an inexperienced Dutch crew. A sudden storm drove the ship onto a sandbank, and 235 were drowned.

The Napoleonic Wars

An expedition in 1801, under Sir Ralph Abercromby, drove Napoleon's forces out of Egypt. The 23rd, which was in Sir John Moore's Brigade, were amongst the first to land. Fixing bayonets, they rushed up the sandy hills and drove the French from them, thus ensuring the safe landing of the rest of the army which led to the surrender of Alexandria and complete victory. In recognition of their conduct the troops received the thanks of Parliament and permission to bear the Sphinx on their Colours with the honour 'Egypt'.

After Egypt, the regiment returned to Gibraltar and thence to England. In 1807 they took part in the seizure of the Danish fleet at Copenhagen, and in 1808 were stationed in Nova Scotia. In January 1809, they were part of a successful expedition sent to take the island of Martinique in the West Indies where they captured a French eagle standard, one of four surrendered when Fort Bourbon capitulated. They returned to Nova Scotia where they remained until 1810.

Meanwhile, in 1804, the regiment was instructed to raise a second battalion. Initially stationed in England, in 1808 it was despatched to Portugal to reinforce the army of Sir John Moore, who was supporting Spanish guerrillas against the French. Learning that the former had been routed, and that Napoleon, with a vastly superior army, intended to envelop and rout the

British, General Moore began his famous retreat to Corunna. The men suffered terribly from a lack of supplies in the snow-covered mountains but, thanks to their discipline, Corunna was reached. The next day, when the army was embarked, the rearguard was commanded by Captain Thomas Fletcher of the 23rd. Being the last to leave, Fletcher pocketed the keys with which his corporal had locked the gates, and to this day the keys of Corunna, with the marks where a bayonet was used to turn them, may be seen in the Regimental Museum in Caernarfon Castle. Shortly after its return from Portugal, the 2nd Battalion took part in the expedition to capture the French fleet at Antwerp. It failed, and the troops were brought home, seriously weakened by sickness. Thus ended the war services of the 2nd Battalion which was disbanded in 1814 on the reduction of the army.

In November 1810, the 1st Battalion left Nova Scotia to join Wellington's army in Portugal, where the Peninsular War was hanging in the balance. The 23rd, together with the 1st and 2nd Battalions The Royal Fusiliers, were in the Fusilier Brigade which formed part of Cole's 4th Division. On 16th May 1811, an allied army under Beresford was drawn up near Albuhera. The French attacked and seized some high ground from which they were able to rake the whole British position. Two counter attacks failed and retreat appeared almost inevitable when the 4th Division was brought up as a last resort. Emerging through the midst of the smoke they met with a fearful discharge of grape and in the words of Napier: 'The fuzileer battalions, struck by the iron tempest, reeled and staggered like sinking ships; but suddenly and sternly recovering they closed on their terrible enemies, and then was seen with what a strength and majesty the British soldier fights ... Nothing could stop that astonishing infantry ... their dreadful volleys swept away the head of every formation'. In the battle, the 23rd suffered 340 casualties.

Waterloo

The regiment had earned another eight Battle Honours in the Peninsula before Napoleon was forced to abdicate in April 1814. The peace, however, was short-lived for he soon escaped from Elba and, on 18th June 1815, Wellington and Napoleon faced each other at Waterloo. Just before the battle Wellington wrote, 'I saw the 23rd the other day, and I never saw a regiment in such order. They are not strong, but it was the most complete and handsome military body I ever looked at'. Starting the battle in reserve, it was not long before they were engaged and they took part in the final rout of the Imperial Guard, in which their highly regarded commanding officer, Colonel Henry Walton Ellis, was mortally wounded. As a reward for the victory, every private soldier received a medal and prize money of £2 11s 4d (£2.62). The defeat of Napoleon at Waterloo brought peace once again, and this time it was almost 40 years before Britain was involved in another European war. The regiment served with the army of occupation in France until 1818, and then spent five years in Ireland before being posted to Gibraltar (1823–7) and Portugal (1827–34).

Canada

The Battalion remained in England for two years before proceeding to Ireland. In 1838, it sailed for Canada where, in 1842, it was joined by the newly raised Reserve Battalion. In the following year, the 1st Battalion left Canada for the West Indies, where it remained until it returned to England, via Canada, in 1848. The 2nd Battalion suffered a tragedy in 1850 when the steamer *Commerce*, which was carrying a company on Lake Erie, collided with another ship and sank with the loss of 33, including families. The Officers' Mess silver was also lost. Three years later, the Battalion returned home to be disbanded with personnel being transferred to the 1st Battalion.

The Crimean War

In 1854, the Crimean War broke out between Russia and Turkey, with Britain and France on the side of the latter. In April, the 23rd embarked at Southampton and were amongst the first to land at Kalamita Bay in the Crimea, 35 miles north of Sevastopol. The Royal Welsh Fusiliers formed part of the Light Division. Soon after the advance on Sevastopol began, the allies were threatened by a Russian force drawn up on high ground behind the River Alma, with the 'Great Redoubt' containing fourteen heavy guns, in the centre. This redoubt was the objective of the Light Division. On 20th September, as the 23rd surged up the steep slope towards the redoubt, the ensigns carrying the Colours were killed. Sergeant Luke O'Connor, already badly wounded, seized the Queen's Colour and, dashing forward, succeeded in planting it on the redoubt. In the confusion Captain Edward Bell captured a Russian gun almost single-handedly and took it back to the British lines. A

Russian counter attack drove the Light Division from the redoubt but, reinforced by the 1st Division, they succeeded in recapturing it. The 23rd sustained over 200 casualties in the battle, including the commanding officer Lieutenant-Colonel Chester. Captain Bell and Sergeant O'Connor were both awarded the Victoria Cross, the latter being commissioned in the field.

The siege of Sevastopol, which began in November, was sustained throughout the terrible Russian winter, during which the soldiers suffered appalling hardships, and continued until the city fell on the 8th September 1855. The 23rd took part in the final assault on the Redan which, although it ended in failure, earned the regiment two more Victoria Crosses, awarded to Assistant-Surgeon Sylvester and Corporal Shields who, under heavy fire, brought in the mortally wounded Adjutant. Casualties in the assault totalled 263.

The Indian Mutiny

With the war over, the 23rd returned to Britain, but it was not long before they were again on active service abroad. In 1857, they embarked for China, but the outbreak of the Indian Mutiny caused them to be diverted and they joined Sir Colin Campbell's relieving force near Lucknow. During the evacuation Lieutenant Hackett and Boy George Monger, the latter aged only seventeen, brought in a seriously-wounded corporal whilst 'exposed to a heavy musketry fire'. For this display of gallantry both were awarded the Victoria Cross. In March 1858 the Battalion participated in the recapture of Lucknow, earning high praise for its part in the capture of the Residency with 'the 23rd Fusiliers charging through the gateway, and driving the enemy before them at the point of the bayonet … .' They remained in India until 1869 when they returned to Britain.

Colonial Wars

Meanwhile, in 1858, a second battalion was again formed. In 1873–4 it took part in the expedition under Sir Garnet Wolseley to Asante (Ashanti) on the west coast of Africa. Their task was to punish the Asante people for raiding and plundering settled tribes in the Gold Coast. A long march through dense jungle led to the capital, Kumasi, which was razed to the ground. 'So ended', wrote Wolseley, 'the most horrible war I ever took part in'.

The Royal Welsh Fusiliers 1881–1920

After a tour in Ireland, the 1st Battalion embarked in 1880 for India, where it was to remain for the next sixteen years, two of which were spent on operations in Burma, including the capture of King Theebaw at Mandalay. In 1891 it was on the North West Frontier of India as part of the Hazara Black Mountain Expedition. It returned to Britain in 1896 and was at Pembroke Dock in 1899 when war broke out in South Africa. The 2nd Battalion, following its return from Asante, was stationed in Gibraltar until 1880. After a short tour in Britain, it arrived in Ireland in 1883 where it remained until 1892. In January 1899, it reached Hong Kong via Britain, Malta, and Crete.

The Cardwell Reforms

In 1877, the regiment acquired its first permanent base when the Depot was established at Wrexham. Four years later, under the major reforms instituted by Cardwell, the regiment was reorganised into four battalions. The 1st and 2nd remained as line battalions, and the Royal Denbigh and Merioneth Rifle Militia, and the Royal Carnarvon Rifle Corps became the 3rd and 4th Battalions respectively. It ceased to be the 'Twenty-third' and was henceforth known as 'The Royal Welsh Fusiliers'. The fact that this title, rather than some less appropriate one, was approved was due in no small part to the good offices of Lord Powis, collateral descendant of the founder of the regiment.

Second Boer War

War with the Boers broke out in 1899 and an army corps was despatched to South Africa. The 1st Battalion reached Durban in November where they joined the 6th Fusilier Brigade, part of the column marching to the relief of Ladysmith. Their first major engagement was at Horse Shoe Hill in February 1900, where the commanding officer, Lieutenant-Colonel Thorold, was killed. This was followed by the triumphal entry into Ladysmith on 3rd March. For the rest of the war the Battalion was engaged on anti-guerrilla operations to protect army supply lines from Boer detachments. It was a thankless task that involved prodigious feats of marching in blazing sun and bitter cold, through dust storms, and always short of food and shelter. Peace was signed in May

1902 and in the following year the Battalion returned to England.

Boxer Rebellion

The 2nd Battalion meanwhile had been despatched from Hong Kong to China in June 1900 where the Boxers, a secret society of xenophobes, were besieging the foreigners sheltering in the British Legation in Peking. The Battalion fought alongside the United States Marine Corps at Tientsin and later at the relief of Peking, thus beginning a close relationship that exists to this day. The Battle Honour 'Pekin 1900' is unique to the Royal Welsh Fusiliers as they were the only British infantry regiment present.

In 1901, the regiment was honoured when the Prince of Wales, later King George V, became its first Colonel-in-Chief.

During the short time remaining until the outbreak of the First World War, the 1st Battalion served in Britain and Ireland before being posted to Malta in January 1914. The 2nd Battalion was in India from 1902 until it returned to England in March 1914 having been abroad for eighteen years. When passing Malta, there was an opportunity for officers of both battalions to meet. This was also the year that Major-General Sir Luke O'Connor VC, of Alma fame, was appointed Colonel of the Regiment.

The Great War

The assassination of the heir to the Austrian throne at Sarajevo in June 1914 plunged Europe into war. At the time, the regiment consisted of seven battalions: two regular – the 1st and 2nd, considered by many to be élite battalions; the 3rd (Special Reserve) Battalion and four Territorial battalions – the 4th, 5th, 6th and 7th. By 1917, that number had risen to 40 battalions, of which over half saw active service abroad. It is impossible in the space available to do more than give the briefest indication of the part played by the regiment in the war.

The 2nd Battalion, recently returned to Britain from India, was the first to be engaged in Europe, at Mons in August 1914. The 1st Battalion followed in October, and by the end of the month it had been virtually annihilated. In November, they were joined in France by the 1/4th (Denbighshire) Battalion. In the meantime, Lord Kitchener had called for 100,000 volunteers, and Lloyd George and other prominent Welshmen determined to raise a Welsh Army

Corps. Such were the numbers who flocked to the recruiting offices that the Territorial Force battalions formed second and third line battalions, and 'service' battalions were raised from scratch, two of which were enlisted in London.

In May 1915, the 1st Battalion played a distinguished part in the battle of Festubert in which Company Sergeant Major Barter, together with eight men, seized and held 500 yards of trench. The Battalion suffered 550 casualties and Barter was awarded the Victoria Cross.

Meanwhile, the landing at Gallipoli had got off to an inauspicious start in April. Lieutenant-Colonel Charles Doughty-Wylie was awarded a posthumous Victoria Cross at Sedd-el-Bahr when, as a staff officer and armed only with a cane, he led a disparate group of soldiers against a key Turkish position and was killed as it was overrun. The 8th (Service) Battalion landed at Anzac Cove in June in support of the Australian and New Zealand Army Corps, and they were followed in August at Suvla Bay by 53rd (Welsh) Division which included the 1/5th, 1/6th and 1/7th Battalions.

During 1915, seven more Service Battalions, the 9th, 10th, 13th, 14th, 15th, 16th and 17th, arrived in France, the last five as part of the 38th (Welsh) Division. The 11th (Service) Battalion went to Macedonia (Salonika) in November where it was engaged alongside the Serbs against Austrians, Germans and Bulgarians until the end of the war in an inhospitable terrain made worse by the presence of malarial mosquitoes.

In 1916, ten battalions were engaged in the battle of the Somme, including those in the 38th Division, which fought with great heroism at Mametz Wood. By the time the Germans had been cleared from the wood, the Royal Welsh losses amounted to well over 1,000 men, and included four out of five commanding officers. On 20th July, Corporal Joseph Davies and Private Albert Hill, both of the 10th Battalion, were awarded Victoria Crosses for their gallantry in attacking, killing and driving off superior numbers of Germans at Delville Wood.

In February 1916, the 8th Battalion was sent to Mesopotamia (Iraq) as part of the force involved in the abortive attempt to relieve the troops besieged at Kut al Amara. It remained in Mesopotamia until the end of the war.

In Europe, 1917 was marked by the battles of 3rd Ypres and Cambrai. Nine battalions fought at Ypres, including the five with 38th Division which distinguished itself at Pilckem Ridge, where Corporal James Davies of the 13th Battalion was awarded a posthumous Victoria Cross for capturing two supposedly impregnable pill-boxes with bayonet and grenade. At Cambrai, the first time that massed tanks were used, the 19th, a bantam battalion (men under 5′ 3″ – 160cms in height), upheld the regiment's reputation for steadiness whilst suffering 370 casualties. In southern Europe, the Italian army was shattered by an Austro-German assault at Caporetto in November 1917. The 1st Battalion were part of the reinforcements sent to bolster the Italian front.

The German spring offensive that opened in March 1918 destroyed much of the Fifth Army. In the initial stages, the 9th Battalion suffered over 450 casualties and the 4th, which was subjected to a mustard-gas bombardment, nearly 300. The former went on to fight with great tenacity at Lys, Bailleul, Kemmel and Scherpenberg, despite being reduced to a skeleton three times in three months.

In Palestine, the 24th and 25th Battalions took part in the capture of Jericho before being sent to France as reinforcements. The 1/5th, 1/6th and 1/7th Battalions fought at Gaza and Tell 'Asur, and went on to serve in General Allenby's final offensive and defeat of the Turks.

In Italy, the 1st Battalion was at the crossing of the Piave, and in the battle of Vittorio Veneto which led to the rout of the Austrian army.

Back in France, the German offensive ran out of steam and in July the allies began to strike back. Corporal Weale, 14th Battalion and Lance Sergeant Waring, 25th Battalion, the latter posthumously, were awarded Victoria Crosses in the closing stages of the war. Sergeant Waring's award was the second Victoria Cross to a soldier of this former dismounted yeomanry battalion.

The cost of the war was enormous. Almost 10,000 officers and men gave their lives and in so doing an amazing 88 Battle Honours were won by the regiment.

The Royal Welch Fusiliers
1920–2006

[Official approval by the Army Board was given on 27th January 1920 for the re-instatement of the spelling 'Welch']

The Inter-War years

Very quickly, the regiment was reduced to its two regular battalions as others were disbanded and it was soon back to business as usual. The 1st Battalion, after re-forming at Oswestry, was sent overseas to India where life was little different to what it had been before the war, with drill, marching and sport occupying the time. Ireland, where the situation was deteriorating rapidly, required reinforcements, and the 2nd Battalion arrived there in 1919 and remained until December 1922. The tour was marred by the tragic loss of Major GL Compton-Smith DSO, who had commanded the 10th Battalion in 1917. He was kidnapped and shot by *Sinn Fein* in April 1921. In a note discovered sometime later he wrote, 'I should like my death to lessen rather than increase the bitterness which exists between England and Ireland. I have been treated with great kindness and ... have learned to regard Sinn Feiners rather as mistaken idealists than as a 'Murder Gang'.'

From Ireland, the 2nd Battalion moved to Pembroke Dock and then, in 1926, joined the British Army of the Rhine at Bingen, remaining there until the final withdrawal in 1929. Returning briefly to Tidworth, they received in 1930 a visit from Lieutenant-Commander John Philip Sousa, the American composer, who presented the regiment with the score of his march *The Royal Welch Fusiliers* in honour of its close relationship with the United States Marine Corps. In 1931 the battalion went to Gibraltar.

The 1st Battalion, meanwhile, had been sent to the North West Frontier of India where the Mahsuds were causing trouble in Waziristan. The battalion suffered many casualties from snipers as they picqueted routes and escorted convoys. In one such action, at Split Hill Picquet, in February 1923, no less than four soldiers were awarded Military Medals for rescuing wounded comrades under fire. Shortly after this the battalion returned to India and was pleased to learn that the War Office had approved of the use of the rank 'Fusilier' for private soldiers. When the tour in India ended in 1930 the battalion was sent to the Sudan, with one company detached to Cyprus. In

October 1931 a revolt broke out in Cyprus and the Governor's house was burnt to the ground. C Company, the only troops on the island, managed to restore order before reinforcements could arrive by air. On their way home in April 1932, the two battalions met at Gibraltar and the officers were able to dine together for the first time since 1914 in Malta.

The 1st Battalion remained in England until the outbreak of war in 1939, and endured the frustrations of trying to train using taxis as armoured cars and rattles to represent machine guns. The 2nd Battalion, which reached Hong Kong in 1934, was called upon to go to Shanghai in 1937 as part of a multi-national force formed to protect the International Settlements which the Sino-Japanese war threatened to engulf. Whilst there, the close links with the United States Marine Corps were renewed. By the end of 1938, the battalion was in India.

The Second World War

The 1st Battalion, as part of the British Expeditionary Force, fought in North West Europe in 1940. Overwhelmed by the Germans, and with their Commanding Officer, Lieutenant-Colonel Harrison, killed, four officers and 263 men were evacuated from Dunkirk. The battalion had suffered nearly 500 casualties, many becoming prisoners of war. Meanwhile, Nº. 2 Independent Company (a precursor of the later Commandos), under the command of Major Hugh Stockwell, with a significant number of Royal Welchmen, participated in the Norway campaign in May 1940.

The 2nd Battalion returned from India in July 1940 and two years later took part in the capture of Madagascar from the Vichy French. In early 1943, it returned to India, thus joining the 1st Battalion which had arrived in the previous year. The latter first saw action against the Japanese at Donbaik in Burma in March 1943. In a battle which, according to General Slim, should never have been fought, he said that '… The last and final assault … was led by the Royal Welch Fusiliers and on that day they showed valour which I think has rarely been surpassed …'. The battalion casualties amounted to thirteen officers and 149 other ranks. It returned to India, and in April and May 1944 fought in the bloody battle for the relief of Kohima, in Assam. It went on to Burma where it was engaged until the end of the war.

The 2nd Battalion operated in North Arakan during the first half of 1944 and then went to northern Burma where it was engaged in clearing the 'Railway Corridor'.

In 1942, the 10th Battalion was converted to the parachute role as 6th (Royal Welch) Parachute Battalion. They served as infantry on the Adriatic flank of the Italian campaign, and at Cassino, before taking part in the airborne landings in the south of France in August 1944. Two months later they dropped near Athens and became involved in ending the Greek Civil War.

The three Territorial battalions, the 4th, 6th and 7th, landed in Normandy in June 1944 as part of the 53rd (Welsh) Division. They received a bloody baptism of fire at Evrecy in July. They fought across France, Belgium, and in Holland where they were engaged in the successful battle for 's-Hertogenbosch, and went on to the Reichswald, the Rhine crossing and the pursuit across Germany, ending the war in the Hamburg area.

The regiment's casualties during the war included over 1,200 killed. In addition to the two Regular, three Territorial and one Parachute battalion that saw service overseas, at home there were two Territorial, five Home Defence and twenty-six Home Guard battalions, all of which bore the regiment's name and wore the Flash.

1945–2006

Having been brought up to strength in Wrexham in 1946, the 1st Battalion was sent to join the British Army of the Rhine in Germany where it remained until 1951. During its tour it spent a year in Berlin at the time of the 'Airlift', when all but aerial access to Berlin was denied by the Russians. At the end of the war the 2nd Battalion went to Japan as part of the army of occupation. After a tour in Malaya (1947–8), it returned to Britain to be disbanded.

With the impetus given to independence movements as a result of the war, internal security duties became an increasing part of the army's life. In 1951, the 1st Battalion arrived in Jamaica and companies were detached elsewhere in the Caribbean. It played a significant part in disaster relief following the hurricane in Jamaica in August. Whilst based in the West Indies, 18 soldiers and dependents lost their lives when an early trooping flight crashed off Newfoundland.

The start of the Korean War led to an army expansion and the 2nd Battalion was re-formed in 1952, and the following year went to Germany.

Returning to the UK in 1954, it was joined by the 1st and 4th Battalions at a Presentation of Colours ceremony by HM The Queen. Immediately afterwards, the 2nd Battalion left for Korea, but its destination was changed en route and it was diverted to Malaya to fight the communist terrorists. When its tour ended it was again disbanded.

The 1st Battalion, which had been in Germany and Berlin, went to Cyprus in 1958 to help combat the EOKA terrorist campaign for union with Greece. The battalion was conspicuously successful in eliminating terrorists from its area. Just over three years in Bulford was followed by a tour as a mechanised battalion in Iserlohn and Minden in Germany, and a six-month United Nations tour in Cyprus.

After two years at Honiton, the battalion was posted in 1969 to Hong Kong, and spent many weeks guarding the Sino-Hong Kong border at a time of much tension during the period of the cultural revolution. In 1972 it went to Northern Ireland for the first of many anti-terrorist tours of duty which have dominated the life of the army since 1969. Others followed in 1974, 1975, 1976, 1977, 1978, 1981, 1986, 1987–9, 1993, 1996, 1998–2000 and 2005–06. All have been most successful, but none more so than in 1981 when, following a particularly difficult tour, members of the battalion were awarded a DSO, MBE, DCM, MC, MM, six Mentions in Despatches, and nine GOC's Commendations.

From 1978 to 1982 the Battalion was based in Lemgo, Germany. On its return to England it became the demonstration battalion at the School of Infantry, Warminster. In October 1985, the battalion moved to Tern Hill in Shropshire. Whilst based there they undertook a six-month garrison tour of duty in the Falkland Islands. A residential tour of Northern Ireland, based Ballykinler followed. In 1989, because of operational commitments in the Province, only two companies were released to take part in the Tercentenary celebrations of the regiment. Later, in July, the battalion went to Berlin where they witnessed the end of the Cold War, and the removal of 'The Wall'. Whilst in Berlin, they won the BAOR Rugby Cup for an unprecedented three consecutive times. After two years in Tidworth (1992–4), the battalion moved to RAF Brawdy in Pembrokeshire. It was the first time since 1926 that a regular battalion of the regiment had served in Wales.

On 1st March 1995, the 1st Battalion, which had just joined UNPROFOR in war-torn Bosnia, assumed responsibility for Gorazde, Kiseljak and Bugojno. It carried out its extremely difficult task of protecting the population until the ending of the Cessation of Hostilities Agreement at the beginning of May, and the NATO bombing of Bosnian Serb positions, made it impossible. On 28th May, 33 members of the battalion were taken hostage by the Bosnian Serbs. The subject of their safety dominated the news until the last batch was released on 16th June. HM The Queen visited the Rear Party in Brawdy during the crisis and spoke with the families of the hostages. Whilst in Bosnia the battalion often used Welsh for security to communicate orders, as had been done fifty years earlier in Burma. On 28th August, and not without difficulty, the last elements evacuated Gorazde, and within a matter of days the battalion was reunited in Wales. Awards for the tour included a DSO, a CGC, three MCs, two MBEs, seven Mentioned in Despatches, and numerous other commendations.

The 1st Battalion moved to Chepstow in December 1995. In May 1996, it was proud to receive new Colours from Her Majesty The Queen, its Colonel-in-Chief. The soldiers of the Second World War were not forgotten when, in November 1997, a regimental memorial was unveiled at Saint-Venant, Pas de Calais, to commemorate those involved with the British Expeditionary Force (1940) and then, in July 1998, a memorial was erected at Evrecy, Normandy to remember those who served and died with 4th, 6th and 7th Battalions during the Normandy campaign (June–August 1944). On the sports field, the 1st Battalion won the Army Rugby Cup and the Infantry Cricket Championship in 2000. The 1st Battalion, which had moved to Tern Hill Shropshire (2000–02) after a two-year resident battalion posting in Ballykelly, Northern Ireland, was deployed from Aldershot operationally in April 2004 to Basra on Operation Telic 4. The awards for the tour included one OBE, three MCs, five Mentions in Despatches and two commendations.

In December 2004, The Chief of the General Staff, General Sir Mike Jackson, announced changes the structure of the infantry. The rationale behind the changes is based on the operational need for more agile, deployable and flexible force. Single battalion regiments will move towards a larger regimental structure consisting of two or more battalions and same time the number of individual infantry battalions would be reduced by four. Following discussions between the Colonels of Regiments within the Prince of Wales's Division, it was announced that the 1st Battalion Royal Welsh Fusiliers would form the 1st Battalion of a new, larger regiment with the title 'The Royal Welsh'. The change would take effect on 1st March 2006. This change, over 300 years since the regiment had been raised, was tinged with much sorrow as the Royal Welch Fusiliers was one of only five infantry regiments of the British Army never to have been amalgamated.

Section 5

24th Regiment of Foot
1689–1881

Early Days – Dering's Regiment

It is often said that if one gets off to a good start one never looks back. Dering's Regiment, later to become known as the 24th Regiment, is a good example of the truth in that saying.

On the 8th March 1689, King William issued a commission to Sir Edward Dering to raise a regiment of foot. The first muster took place on 28th March 1689, and in August that year the new regiment embarked for its first campaign in Ireland, under the command of General Lord Schomberg. They served throughout the three years of a campaign of great hardship and sickness, which ended in the fall of Limerick and the withdrawal of the French in August 1692.

Marlborough's Wars

In November 1700, Charles II of Spain died, leaving his dominions in Spain, the Netherlands and the Americas to Philip of Anjou, grandson of Louis XIV of France. King William immediately ordered the twelve regiments in Ireland to embark for Holland. The regiment, under Colonel William Seymour, sailed from Cork in June 1701.

In February 1702, Seymour transferred to the King's Own Regiment and John Churchill, Duke of Marlborough, Commander-in-Chief of King William's forces on the Continent and one of England's greatest soldiers, took over as Colonel of the Regiment. The regiment served throughout the War of the Spanish Succession and fought at the famous battles of Blenheim (1704), Ramillies (1706), Oudenarde (1708) and Malplaquet (1709).

Marlborough was the first senior commander who really cared for the welfare of his troops. This Marlborough tradition, maintained over the years, has helped to foster the family spirit which has always been a marked feature of the regiment and has led to many outstanding achievements and the award of 23 Victoria Crosses to its soldiers.

American War of Independence

Early in 1776, two expeditions were sent from England to quell the rebellion in North America. The main force, under Sir William Howe, was directed against New York, where he was to await the arrival of the second force which would join him after relieving Quebec. By the time the 24th Regiment arrived in Canada, Quebec had been relieved and the Americans were in full retreat to the border. The advance south under General Burgoyne began in June 1777 and continued for two months. The 24th Regiment, as part of the advance guard, were frequently in action. By 17th September 1777, Burgoyne's army had reached Stillwater, near Saratoga, where 10,000 Americans under General Gates were entrenched. Through lack of provisions and reinforcements, Burgoyne found his position untenable and withdrew. The force was soon overtaken by the Americans and Burgoyne was forced to surrender at Saratoga. The campaign ended in disaster, but the 24th had no reason to be anything but proud of the part they played in it by showing the true soldierly qualities of hard marching, initiative, self-reliance and good discipline.

In 1782, the 24th Regiment was instructed to style itself the 24th (2nd Warwickshire) Regiment of Foot, and it was under this title that the regiment was known for the next 100 years.

24th (2nd Warwickshire) Regiment of Foot
1782–1881

The Napoleonic Wars

In June 1801, five regiments, including the 24th Regiment, were sent to Egypt to reinforce the British force which, under General Hutchinson, was fighting the French. They arrived in time to take part in the capture of Alexandria which ended the campaign as a result of which, the 24th, together with the other regiments engaged, were awarded the Sphinx, superscribed 'Egypt' which was later an insignia on the Regimental Colour and the collar badge of the regiment.

In August 1805, the battalion sailed under Sir David Baird, later to become Colonel of 24th, to the Cape of Good Hope. By January 1806, the Dutch forces had surrendered at Blaauwberg and the Cape was secured.

In September 1804, a second battalion was raised which took part in Wellington's great victories in Spain, gaining nine Battle Honours for the regiment. The most significant and hardest of these was Talavera, in July 1809, when the 2/24th held their line, suffered many casualties, but allowed the Foot Guards to re-form in the rear and secure a famous victory for Wellington.

India: The Second Sikh War

In 1849, the 1st Battalion of the 24th fought as part of General Sir Hugh Gough's Army of the Punjab at Chillianwallah in the Second Sikh War. On this occasion its conduct inspired General Colin Campbell to write: 'It is impossible for any troops to have surpassed the gallantry displayed in this attack. This single regiment actually broke the enemy's line and took the large number of guns to their front'. In 1866, a regimental memorial was erected in the grounds of the Royal Hospital Chelsea to remember those who had been killed at Chillianwallah on 13th January 1849. It is the only regiment to be honoured there in this way.

The Andaman Islands

In 1867, the 2/24th was stationed at Rangoon, with a detachment of 3 officers and 100 soldiers in the Andaman Islands. In May that year the crew of a British ship was reported to have been murdered by the natives of the Little Andaman and a party was sent to investigate. On arrival at the reputed place of the massacre, two boats were put ashore but, due to the heavy surf, only one reached the shore. The landing party discovered the bodies of the murdered crew, but hostile natives soon appeared. The shore-party's ammunition was soon exhausted in their efforts to escape and re-float their boat when it was upset in the surf. Several attempts were made to rescue them, but finally the second boat, crewed by Assistant-Surgeon Douglas and Privates Bell, Cooper, Griffiths and Murphy, which had remained off-shore, managed to pick up the men by making two trips through the difficult waters and thus saving the soldiers from certain death. The crew of the rescue boat were later to receive the Victoria Cross – the first members of the 24th to be given this recently established but much coveted decoration.

The South African campaigns

Both 1st and 2nd Battalions of the 24th were engaged in the Ninth Frontier War in the Eastern Cape in 1877–8 and the subsequent war against the Zulus in 1879. On 22nd January 1879, five companies of the 1st Battalion and one company of the 2nd, in camp at Isandlwana, were attacked by a great mass of Zulus. Surrounded and greatly outnumbered, they fought desperately but were finally overwhelmed when the supply of ammunition failed. Twenty-one officers and 575 men of the regiment perished that day and only ten escaped with their lives.

When it was evident that all was lost, Lieutenants Melvill and Coghill were ordered to save the Queen's Colour of the 1st Battalion. They fought their way through to the Buffalo River, where both were killed. Some two weeks later, the Colour was recovered from the muddy waters of the Buffalo and restored to the battalion. The families of Lieutenants Melvill and Coghill later received their posthumous Victoria Crosses.

Meanwhile, B Company 2nd/24th, under Lieutenant Gonville Bromhead was at Rorke's Drift, some ten miles from the scene of the disaster. That same afternoon, the victorious Zulus swept on and some 4,000 of them launched a series of fierce attacks on the tiny garrison at Rorke's Drift. The attacks continued until the early hours of the following morning but were all beaten off. This action undoubtedly saved Natal from invasion. Of the 24th, Lieutenant Bromhead and six NCOs and men were awarded the Victoria Cross for their gallantry at Rorke's Drift. No other regiment has been awarded seven Victoria Crosses for a single action.

On the return of the 1st Battalion from South Africa, Queen Victoria expressed a wish to see the Isandlwana Colour that had been recovered from Buffalo river, and with her own hands placed upon it a wreath of immortelles (dried flowers), directing that a silver replica should always be borne round the staff of the Queen's Colour of both battalions, to commemorate the devotion of Lieutenants Melvill and Coghill and the noble defence of Rorke's Drift by B Company of the 2nd Battalion. This Queen's Colour was carried by the 1st Battalion until 1933 and now hangs in the Regimental Chapel in Brecon Cathedral. Beneath it, in an oaken case, is Queen Victoria's original wreath.

The South Wales Borderers
1881–1969

The Cardwell Reforms

By 1873, the 24th Regiment was recruiting mainly from the Welsh counties of Cardigan, Radnor, Brecknock, Montgomery and Monmouth) with its training depot in Brecon. It was therefore logical that in 1881, when the infantry was given territorial titles, it should assume the title of The South Wales Borderers. Shortly after this, the Volunteer battalions of Monmouthshire, as well as those of Brecknock, Radnor and Montgomery were affiliated to the regiment. It was at this time that the 24th lost their grass-green facings for white. Happily, this distinction was restored to the regiment in 1905.

The Second Boer War

After 'Black Week' in December 1899, the 2nd Battalion was sent to South Africa. The Boer War also gave a first-ever chance for the Volunteer and Militia units of the South Wales Borderers to see active service overseas. The success of the Volunteers led to the creation of the Monmouthshire Regiment (TF) in 1908, from the 2nd, 3rd and 4th Volunteer battalions of the South Wales Borderers.

The Great War

In the First World War, the 24th raised 21 battalions, gained six Victoria Crosses and was awarded 74 Battle Honours, of which none was better earned than Gheluvelt on 31st October 1914, where the 1st Battalion, alongside the 2nd Battalion The Welsh Regiment, withstood the German onslaught and enabled 2nd Battalion The Worcestershire Regiment to launch their famous counter-attack, thus halting the whole German offensive towards the coast.

Also in 1914, but on the other side of the world in northern China, the 2nd Battalion took part with the Japanese in the capture of the German treaty port of Tsingtao and thereby gained a Battle Honour unique in the British Army. The 2nd Battalion returned via Hong Kong to England in early 1915, only to form part of the 29th Division which was sent to land at Cape Helles on the Gallipoli peninsula on 25th April 1915. After the failure of the Dardanelles campaign, the 29th Division was withdrawn merely to arrive in France in

March 1916. Its first big action was on 1st July 1916, the opening day of the great battle of the Somme, when it attacked the impregnable position at Beaumont Hamel. The leading line of the 2nd Battalion, advancing south of the village, was mown down by machine-gun fire in the first few minutes, losing 11 officers and 235 men killed and missing, and 4 officers and 149 men wounded, out of a total of 21 officers and 578 men. Some gallant fellows reached the German wire 300 yards away, but neither here nor at other places did the Division's attack succeed. The battalion was soon re-formed and after periods in various parts of the Line fought most gallantly at Monchy Le Preux during the Arras offensive in April and May 1917, where Sergeant White was awarded a posthumous Victoria Cross for magnificent leadership and self-sacrifice.

In 1916, the 4th (Service) Battalion was involved in operations to relieve General Townsend's force besieged at Kut al Amara in Mesopotamia (Iraq). On 4th April, the British attacked the Hanna position. The battalion pushed on under heavy machine-gun fire over ground devoid of cover and, despite severe losses, reached a line about 800 yards from the Turkish trenches. During the advance an officer fell and one of his men, going to his help, was hit and disabled. Captain Angus Buchanan thereupon dashed out from behind cover and not only carried the officer in, despite a heavy fire, but, going out again, also brought in the private, for which gallantry he was awarded the Victoria Cross. A few days later, on 8th April, came the night assault on the Turkish position at Sannaiyat, with the 4th Battalion in the front line. The attack failed with heavy losses, but the regiment gained another Victoria Cross of the battalion; Private James Fynn crept out in broad daylight to two men who were lying within 300 yards of the Turkish line, bandaged them and brought them in.

For its epic actions on 18th September 1918, the 7th Battalion were awarded the *Croix de Guerre* by the French for their attack on the Grand Couronné in Macedonia; only eleven units of the British Army have been given this distinct honour. The Commanding Officer, Lieutenant-Colonel Daniel Burges, was awarded the Victoria Cross.

During the Great War, 5,777 soldiers of the South Wales Borderers and 2,430 soldiers of the Monmouthshire Regiment gave their lives for their country.

Between the Wars

The years between the wars were not particularly peaceful as both battalions were involved in the trouble spots of the Empire: the 1st Battalion served in Egypt, Palestine, Hong Kong and on the North West Frontier of India; the 2nd Battalion served in India, Malta, Palestine and finally in Northern Ireland. In 1929, the 'Corps of The South Wales Borderers' was officially recognised as comprising the two regular battalions and the three battalions of The Monmouthshire Regiment.

The Second World War

In 1939, the 1st Battalion was stationed in India and 2nd in Northern Ireland. Neither was to be involved in the British Expeditionary Force sent to France in September 1939 to stop the German forces' advance through Europe. However, when the Germans invaded the neutral counties of Norway and Denmark in March 1940, the 2nd Battalion joined 24th (Guards) Brigade to form part of a small allied force sent to aid Norway north of the Arctic Circle. The battalion arrived in mid-April and advanced towards Narvik with other allied troops. In early May, the battalion successfully beat off a German attack, but in mid-May was withdrawn. The whole force was withdrawn at the end of May. The expedition had failed largely because the Germans had full command of the air and allied forces lacked the training and equipment to fight under Arctic conditions. The 2nd Battalion lost six dead and thirteen wounded, and two DCMs were later awarded for gallantry.

Soldiers from the South Wales Borderers were selected to support the newly created Parachute Regiment in one of the most daring operations of the Second War when they landed in occupied France during the night 27/28 February 1942 to capture a German radar site at Bruneval, near Le Harve, and seize vital parts for subsequent intelligence evaluation. The raid was entirely successful and a welcome morale boost for the British public.

At home, the Brecknockshire Battalion was a draft-finding unit and the 1st South Wales Borderers, after a difficult time in the Western Desert in 1942, amalgamated with the 4th Monmouthshires, served as a training unit, both vital if unexciting roles.

In June 1944, the 2nd Battalion had the distinction of being the only Welsh battalion to land on the Normandy Beaches on D-Day, and together with the

2nd and 3rd Monmouths fought throughout the North-West Europe campaign until VE Day, whilst the 6th Battalion was one of the outstanding battalions in Burma and of particular note was its action at the Mayu Tunnels in February 1944 where railway tunnels, used as a storage depot by the Japanese, were destroyed by a determined company assault and the inspirational use of a Sherman tank.

An end and a new beginning

The post-war years saw the regiment dealing with illegal Jewish immigrants in Palestine and Cyprus; curbing the Shifta's activities in Eritrea; fighting communist terrorists in Malaya, after which Field-Marshal Sir Gerald Templer wrote '... there has been no better regiment in Malaya during the ten years of the emergency and very few as good ... .' While the battalion was based in Hong Kong (1963–6), three platoons were in turn deployed to Borneo on counter-insurgency operations and were attached to 1st Battalion Gordons, 1st Battalion Scots Guards and 1st Battalion Durham Light Infantry respectively. The Borderers final operational tour was policing the Ma'alla district of Aden in 1967.

As a result of the 1967 Defence Review, drastic cuts in the armed forces were proposed. The Welsh Brigade was to be reduced by one battalion. Fortunately, an interchange of officers and senior ranks between regiments in the brigade had occurred for many years, so the amalgamation of the South Wales Borderers with the Welch Regiment, although tinged with much sadness, enabled the newly formed Royal Regiment of Wales to capitalise immediately on the traditions and soldierly qualities of two fine Welsh regiments.

Section 6

41st Regiment
1719–1831

Colonel Edmund Fielding's Regiment of Invalids

A forerunner of the later veteran battalions, the regiment was raised from out-pensioners of the Royal Hospital Chelsea for garrison duty at home. Known originally as 'Colonel Edmund Fielding's Regiment of Invalids', its colonel was, like many of the pensioners, a veteran of Marlborough's wars. Many were partially disabled, but all were considered capable of performing the duties required of a soldier in garrison. On 1st July 1751, the regiment was numbered 41st and re-designated as the 41st Foot (or Invalids). Its service was confined mainly to the Portsmouth garrison with detachments at Plymouth and in the Channel Islands.

On 11th December 1787, the Invalids character of the regiment was abandoned and the out-pensioners discharged. Re-categorised as a marching regiment of the line, younger men were recruited in preparation for active or general service at home or abroad. The strong links with the Royal Hospital Chelsea continue to this day.

Ireland and the West Indies

A great deal of time was devoted to recruiting in 1788, a year which, on 23rd January, saw Lieutenant the Honourable Arthur Wesley (Wellesley) exchange from the 76th Foot into the regiment. Wellesley, afterwards the Duke of Wellington, was a 'bird of passage' who moved on into the 12th Light Dragoons within 17 months, but his connection was always proudly valued by the regiment.

In 1793, the 41st embarked at Cork for the West Indies where they were present at the capture of Martinique, St Lucia and Guadeloupe, and in operations in San Domingo (Haiti/Dominican Republic). In 1796, surviving private soldiers were transferred to the 17th Foot. The officers and NCOs disembarked at Portsmouth in October of the same year.

Canada – The Anglo-American War of 1812–14
France – With the Army of Occupation 1815

In August 1799, the 41st embarked at Cork for Canada. A declaration of war by the United States in 1812 destroyed any hopes of an early homeward passage. The corps gained the distinction of being amongst the small number of British line regiments which, with Canadian support, saved Canada from being absorbed into the United States of America. During a difficult campaign, the 41st was reinforced by a 2nd Battalion (raised in 1812). United as one battalion, they were actively engaged until the war ended in December 1814. In June 1815, the battalion arriving in Spithead was diverted to Belgium and thence to Paris to join Wellington's Army of Occupation. In November, they returned to England and in due course received the battle honours Detroit, Queenstown, Miami and Niagara for their campaign in North America.

41st (The Welsh) Regiment of Foot
1831–81

Campaigning in Burma
The 1st Afghan War

In 1822, the 41st embarked at Gravesend for India and by 1824 was serving with Sir Colin Campbell's expeditionary force to the Kingdom of Ava (now Burma) where, until March 1826, they were involved in the 1st Burma War. That campaign was followed by years of garrison duty in India, a period highlighted mainly by the territorialisation of the regiment as the 41st or The Welsh Regiment of Infantry in February 1831. In 1842, the regiment formed part an Army of Retribution which launched a two-pronged attack on Afghanistan. Included in General Nott's column, its services in the arduous campaign was later marked by the award of the battle honours Candahar, Ghuznee and Cabul. Returning to Britain in 1843, the regiment served in South Wales. In 1845 it moved on to Ireland where it served on garrison duties until 1851.

Garrison Duty at home and abroad

The Crimean War

The 41st embarked from Ireland for the Mediterranean in 1851 where for two years they formed the Ionian Islands' garrison. As part of the British Second Division, the regiment landed in the Crimea in September 1854 and subsequently fought in and gained Battle Honours for the battles of the Alma and Inkerman and the siege of Sebastopol. Two Victoria Crosses (including the first awarded to a Welshman, Captain Hugh Rowlands) and 17 Distinguished Conduct Medals were awarded to members of the 41st for gallantry during the campaign. The regiment disembarked at Portsmouth on 28th July 1856, and the following day were together with other Crimea veterans reviewed by HM Queen Victoria at Aldershot.

The West Indies, India, Aden and Natal

Six months later, the Welsh embarked at Portsmouth for the West Indies to serve in garrison at Trinidad, Barbados and Jamaica where they remained April 1860. At Sheffield in 1862, the regiment received from the Queen a white billygoat from the Royal herd as replacement for its Russian goat which had died in the West Indies. From Ireland in 1865 the regiment embarked for India. Service in the sub-continent was followed in 1874 by a year in the Aden garrison prior to returning to Britain in March 1875. Service at home, which included some time in Pembrokeshire, was followed in 1880 by seven months in the Gibraltar garrison and then service in Natal policing the colony in the aftermath of the Zulu campaign. There, in July 1881, a new territorial system saw the 41st (The Welsh) united with the 69th (South Lincolnshire) Regiment to form respectively the 1st and 2nd Battalions, The Welsh Regiment. The reorganisation saw the Royal Glamorgan Light Infantry Militia become the Regiment's third battalion and four South Wales Rifle Volunteer Corps affiliated as Volunteer battalions of the regiment. A new regimental depot was established at the then recently completed Maindy Barracks in Cardiff.

Section 7

69TH REGIMENT OF FOOT 1758–82

By land and sea

Raised as a 2nd Battalion to the 24th Foot in 1756, the regiment was shortly after its formation placed at the disposal of the Admiralty for service with the Fleet. Re-numbered as a regiment in its own right, the battalion was re-designated as the 69th Foot in April 1758. Although intermittent, its sea service between 1757 and 1800 was extensive. As a result of their 'numbering', the 69th acquired the sobriquet the 'Ups and Downs'.

69TH (SOUTH LINCOLNSHIRE) REGIMENT OF FOOT 1782–1881

Naval honours

The regiment saw service on land in the West Indies, at home, in France and, in 1794, in Corsica. However, it was its service as marines with the Fleet which are best remembered today. On the 12th April 1782, the regiment served as the marines in Hood's division of Admiral Rodney's fleet at the Battle of the Saints, which secured control of the Caribbean for the British. A detachment was present with Howe's fleet at the battle known as the Glorious First of June, 1794. Following service at sea in the Mediterranean, detachments served with distinction with Sir John Jervis's fleet at the Battle of St Vincent on 14th February 1797.

The Welch Regiment was in its day unique in being the only British regiment to carry two naval Battle Honours on its Regimental Colour, namely a Naval Crown, superscribed '12th April 1782', for the Battle of the Saints and the battle honour scroll 'St Vincent' to mark its services on the 14th February 1797. The honours and their uniqueness continue today.

Quatre Bras and Waterloo

A 2nd Battalion of 69th Foot was raised under the Additional Forces Act, July 1803. In March 1814, the 2nd Battalion took part in the disastrous assault on Bergen op Zoom. Later, as part of Halkett's 5th British Brigade, the battalion due to mishandling by the Prince of Orange, was badly cut up at Quatre Bras and lost its King's Colour. On 18th June 1815, the battalion fought at Waterloo and by that service added the Battle Honour 'Waterloo' to the Colour of the 69th Regiment. The 2nd Battalion was in 1816 disbanded as part of a general plan of demobilisation and its remaining personnel absorbed into the 1/69th Foot then serving in India.

India and the East Indies

The 69th disembarked at Madras in July 1805. At Vellore in July 1806, it survived an attack by mutinous sepoys, losing two officers and 80 other ranks. After service in the Travancore campaign of 1809, the regiment was present at the capture of Bourbon (Reunion Island) and Mauritius the following year; and in 1811 was included in Auchmuty's expeditionary force which captured Java. The next fourteen years were spent expanding and consolidating British influence in India, and service in the Mahratta War 1817–20. In February 1826, the 69th disembarked at Gravesend and on 30th May was awarded the Battle Honour 'India' in recognition of its distinguished service in that sub-continent.

The 'Ups and Downs' on colonial service

This period saw the 69th serving on garrison duty in England (1826–31), the West Indies and Demerara, South America (1831–38), Nova Scotia (1839–42) and then England. From 1847 to 1851 the regiment served in Malta before returning to the West Indies in 1851. Back in England in 1857, the Ups and Downs were within six months on their way to Burma and were the first regiment to use the overland route via Egypt to the East. In 1864, the 69th returned to England from India prior to embarking in 1867 for Canada. In 1870, on the United States/Canadian border, the regiment successfully routed an incursion by Fenians into Canadian territory, an action which earned for battalion members the Canada General Service Medal. Later that same year, the 69th moved to Bermuda and in 1873 back to Europe and the Gibraltar garrison. In 1878, the regiment returned to England where, in July 1881, it was re-designated as the 2nd Battalion, The Welsh Regiment.

Section 8

The Welsh Regiment
1881–1920

Natal, Egypt, the Sudan, Malta and at home

In 1886, the 1st Battalion moved from Natal to Egypt where on 20th December 1888, a half battalion commanded by Lieutenant Colonel CC Smyth saw action against a Dervish force at Fort Gemaizah near Suakim. In 1889 the battalion mounted infantry were active against Dervishes in the vicinity of Tosci. After Egypt the battalion moved to Malta and thence to Wales and Pembroke Dock in December 1893. There in March 1895 a disastrous fire resulted in the loss of officers' mess silver and many early manuscript regimental records.

The Second Boer War
The Haldane Reforms

The war in South Africa saw the 1st Battalion disembark at Port Elizabeth in the Eastern Cape in November 1899 to participate in a war where, for the first time, the Regulars of the battalion found themselves supported by Volunteer companies drawn from the four Volunteer battalions of The Welsh Regiment at home in South Wales. In April 1908, the implementation of the Haldane reforms resulted in the 3rd (Militia) Battalion being re-categorised as a Special Reserve battalion and four new battalions for the Territorial Force were created from the Volunteer battalions of the regiment.

Prelude to war

On its return to the United Kingdom from South Africa in 1904, the 1st Battalion enjoyed some home service prior to embarking in December 1909 for service in Egypt and the Sudan. In February 1914, it moved on to India where at the outbreak of the Great War, it was stationed at Chakrata. Ordered back to the United Kingdom, the battalion was brought up to war establishment and embarked for France on 16th January 1915.

The 2nd Battalion embarked for India from England in 1892. After almost fourteen years in the sub-continent, in 1906 the battalion moved to garrison duties in South Africa in 1906, before returning to Britain in 1910. The battalion was for a period stationed at Pembroke Dock, but moved to Bordon just prior to the outbreak of the Great War. It embarked for France on 12th August 1914 where, with the 6th Battalion (TF), it represented the regiment in 'Britain's Contemptible Little Army'.

The Great War

Of the Welsh Regiment's 34 active battalions during the war, 19 saw active service overseas in France, Belgium, Gallipoli, Egypt, Syria, Mesopotamia and Macedonia. Three members of the regiment were awarded the Victoria Cross for valour.

Of special mention was the important role played by the Service battalions of Lloyd George's 'Welsh Army'. In December 1915, the 38th (Welsh) Division, which included new battalions from the Royal Welsh Fusiliers, the South Wales Borderers and the Welsh Regiment, all enlisted in Wales, disembarked in France. The battalions of the Welsh Regiment involved were the 10th, 13th (Rhondda), 14th (Swansea) and 15th (Carmarthen), all part of 115th Brigade. In addition, there were the 16th Welsh (City of Cardiff) and the 19th Welsh (Pioneers). After spells in the Line at Givenchy during the spring of 1916, the Division moved to the River Ancre on 3rd July at the opening of the Battle of the Somme, and both battalions had their first real action in the attack on Mametz Wood. Here they had five days' hard fighting in a thick wood flanked by machine guns. It required skill and determination on the part of all ranks to turn the Germans out, and fine work was done with bomb and bayonet by the courage and initiative of junior leaders. The stiffness of the fighting may be gauged by the casualties sustained by the 38th Division which amounted to 190 officers and 3,803 other ranks, of which 75 officers and 1,598 other ranks belonged to Welsh Regiment – Lieutenant-Colonel J Hayes, 14th Welsh, particularly distinguished himself and several DSOs and MCs, together with 17 Military Medals were awarded to the regiment.

The 9th Welsh, as part of 19th Division, were engaged in three actions, suffering heavily and gaining many awards, but it was 2nd Welsh that took the brunt of the fighting on the Somme being engaged no fewer than five times in heavy fighting for Bazentin and Pozières Ridges, twice in High Wood and at Flers. They lost 32 officers and 859 soldiers and gained 7 MCs, 12 DCMs and 34 MMs. The 6th Welsh had lost 10 officers and 150 soldiers and established their reputation as pioneer battalion second to none.

In July 1917, the 38th Welsh Division was allocated the task of capturing Pilckhem Ridge some five kilometres north of Ypres and, as at the fight for Mametz Wood, the Welsh Regiment and the Royal Welsh Fusilier brigades opened the attack with the Welsh on the right and the Royal Welsh Fusiliers on the left. The attack was entirely successful, the four battalions of the Welsh Regiment gaining their objectives; the 14th and 15th Welsh capturing 'pill boxes' by good tactics and with the Royal Welsh Fusiliers, defeating the famous Prussian *Führer* Guards, known as 'The Cockchafers'. The two brigades had advanced over three kilometres and were now holding the top of the ridge. Two battalions of 115th Brigade passed through them and attacked the 'pill boxes' on the River Steenbeek, but the German artillery now began to have an impact, and B Company 16th Welsh was sent forward and had a rough time but put up a great fight. The 38th Division held the position for three days, after which they were relieved.

Cambrai was one of the last great battles of 1917 and was notable as being the first battle in which the newly-invented tanks were used in large numbers. Employed were the soldiers of 40th Division which contained the bantam battalions of 17th and 18th Welsh, as well as the bantams from 19th Royal Welsh Fusiliers and 12th South Wales Borderers. On one portion of the front lay a large wood on the top of a hill, named Bourlon Wood, which was the key position in that area. On 23 November, the 40th Division was ordered to take this wood. After long hours of fighting and with the assistance of tanks, the whole of the wood was captured. The Germans put in a number of strong counter attacks and for three days the struggle swayed backwards and forwards, the enemy pounding the wood with heavy artillery and drenching it with gas, but the British held firm. The 17th Welsh lost 17 officers and 301 soldiers and 18th Welsh 15 officers and 241 soldiers. Their fight was recognised by the award of 1 DSO, 1 bar to MC, 8 MCs, 6 DCMs, 2 bars to MMs and 27 MMs.

Bulgaria declared war on the Allies in October 1915 and proceeded to invade Serbia, who then called on the British and French for assistance. France sent three divisions and Britain four divisions, amongst which was the 28th

Division from France, which included 1st Welsh (and later the pioneers of 23rd Welsh) and the 27th Division which included 11th Welsh. 1st Welsh held the line in the swampy valley of the River Struma and was so reduced in strength by malarial fever that they could not be used for large-scale operations. 11th Welsh, positioned on higher, healthier ground, carried out a particularly successful raid in October 1916, in which Private Herbert 'Stokey' Lewis was awarded the Victoria Cross. In the final battle of this campaign in Macedonia, on 18th/19th September 1918, 11th Welsh performed magnificently, only one officer and 128 soldiers remaining unwounded out of 324 who began the the offensive. Three DSOs and two MCs were awarded for their fine efforts.

By the end of the conflict in 1918, 7,679 soldiers of the Welsh Regiment had given their lives for their country. Later, the regiment was awarded 70 battle honours, of which ten were selected for display on the King's Colour of the Regular and Territorial Force battalions. In 1919, the Territorial Force and Service battalions stood down and the cadres of the 1st and 2nd Battalions, on being brought up to their established strength at Pembroke Dock, prepared for peacetime service.

The Welch Regiment
1920–69

[Official approval by the Army Board was given on 27th January 1920 for the re-instatement of the spelling 'Welch']

Between the Wars

By 1920, the Regular battalions were as they had been in August 1914, with the 2nd Battalion at home and the 1st Battalion in India.

In 1920–1, the 2nd Battalion saw service in troubled Ireland. Whilst 1923–4 found the 1st Battalion on active service against Waziris on the North West Frontier. In 1927, 1st Welch moved via Aden back to the United Kingdom whilst 2nd Welch embarked for Shanghai and duty with the China Defence Force. From China, 2nd Welch, after service at Singapore, moved on to India where in 1935 it served at Landi Kotal on the North West Frontier. At the close of 1938, the 1st Battalion was stationed at Belfast and the 2nd Battalion at Agra in India.

The Second World War

During the Second World War, eleven battalions of the regiment were active, but only four saw service overseas. The 1st Battalion which, at the outbreak of war was serving in Palestine, served in the Western Desert, Crete, Sicily and Italy, whilst the 2nd Battalion served with the 14th Army in the Burma campaign. After home defence service, the 4th and 1/5th Territorial Army battalions served with the 53rd (Welsh) Division during the 1944–5 campaign in France and North West Europe.

Over 1,100 soldiers gave their lives during the conflict. The regiment was later awarded 22 Battle Honours of which ten were selected for display on the King's Colour of each battalion.

The post-Second World War years

In 1947, the Regular battalions returned to the United Kingdom after years of peacetime and wartime foreign service. In 1948, the 2nd Battalion was disbanded, thus leaving the regiment with only one regular battalion. The 4th and 1/5th Territorial battalions, which had stood down in 1946, were re-formed in 1947 and resumed a programme of peacetime training activities. In 1950, on completion of a training role, the 1st Battalion resumed duties as an active battalion of infantry and was sent to Korea in 1951 to serve under United Nations command in the Commonwealth Division. Its year of service during that conflict brought the Battle Honour 'Korea 1951–52' to the Colours and was followed by a period of service in the Hong Kong garrison.

Thereafter, the battalion, interposed with service at home, was increasingly involved with the British Army of the Rhine (particularly in Berlin when 'The Wall' was built in 1963), in Cyprus (during the EOKA campaign), Libya and again in Hong Kong, in support of the police during the riots at the height of the Chinese Cultural Revolution. In 1968, the Battalion was stationed at Gravesend and undertook public duties in London and in 1969 celebrated the 250th anniversary of its formation.

On 11th June 1969, came amalgamation with the 1st Battalion, The South Wales Borderers to form the 1st Battalion, The Royal Regiment of Wales (24th/41st Foot), thus bringing to a close its 250 years of distinguished independent service.

Section 9

THE ROYAL REGIMENT OF WALES (24TH/41ST FOOT) 1969–2006

Despite its short existence of just over 36 years, 1st Battalion, The Royal Regiment of Wales (24th / 41st Foot) was involved in demanding, challenging, but very interesting and exciting, events in its many and varied postings and operational tours.

Within two months of amalgamation, the battalion was serving in Northern Ireland and was one of the first units to be deployed on the streets of the province when the troubles began in August 1969. At the end of that year, it was posted to Osnabrück in West Germany for four years but returned to Northern Ireland on two occasions for short tours. On one occasion, Lance Corporal Bennett was awarded the George Medal for bravery while under fire.

In 1973, the battalion returned to Belfast for two years as the resident unit, but afterwards, in 1975, had the benefit of an enjoyable two years in Berlin. From 1977 to 1982 it was based in Aldershot, but spent time in Belize and Hong Kong, as well as on exercise in Germany. In 1979, the battalion re-enacted the defence of Rorke's Drift as part of the centenary events at the Cardiff Castle Tattoo. Six months later, it was on public duties mounting Royal Guards at Buckingham Palace and the Tower of London. Towards the end of 1979, 25 soldiers were to play a significant role during Operation AGILA which monitored the fragile ceasefire in Rhodesia (now Zimbabwe) prior to and during that former colony's first all-party elections.

Anti-terrorist duties in Northern Ireland continued to dominate life in the battalion during this period. Of particular note was its deployment to Belfast for an emergency tour in May 1981 following the death of hunger-striker Bobby Sands when soldiers found themselves patrolling the streets of the city alongside the 1st Battalion The Royal Welch Fusiliers. There were further operational tours in the province in 1983–4 and 1986–7. In 1982, the battalion moved to Lemgo in West Germany to begin a six-year tour of duty as a Mechanised Infantry Battalion with battle-group training taking place at Suffield in Canada for six weeks in 1985. In 1988, the battalion returned to Warminster in Wiltshire as the School of Infantry's Demonstration Battalion. In 1989, the regiment held its Tercentenary Parade at Cardiff Castle to celebrate the formation of the regiment in March 1689. In 1990, the battalion arrived in Hong Kong where it deployed to the Sino-Hong Kong border and also carried out anti-smuggling operations with the police. The opportunities to travel, play sport and participate in adventurous training were numerous and overseas deployments took members of the battalion as far as Hawaii, Australia, New Zealand, Borneo and Malaysia.

Three years later, the battalion returned to Britain to be stationed at Tern Hill in Shropshire. From there a company group was deployed to the Falkland Islands and South Georgia on an operational tour. Other companies visited Italy and Jamaica as part of exchange visits.

In early 1994, the battalion changed roles and began an intense period of Northern Ireland training prior to its deployment to Ballykelly in County Londonderry as a resident battalion. In July that year, on 25th anniversary of the appointment of The Prince of Wales as Colonel-in-Chief, a memorable parade and regimental garden party was held in Cardiff Castle at which His Royal Highness was asked to cut the first slice of a large regimental birthday cake.

After a full tour of public duties in London, the 1st Battalion moved to Paderborn in Germany in February 1998 where it took up an armoured infantry role, equipped with Warrior armoured fighting-vehicles, in 1st (UK) Armoured Division, part of NATO's Allied Command Europe (ACE) Rapid Reaction Corps. In 1999 and 2001 it was operationally deployed in Bosnia (Operation PALATINE) and then Kosovo (Operation AGRICOLA). More recently, the 1st Battalion has been involved in two six-month operational tours in Iraq which involved leaving the families in Paderborn. In 2005, the battalion returned to Britain to be based at Tidworth.

The Tercentenary of the battle of Blenheim in 2004 was marked by a special dinner in London, attended by the Colonel-in-Chief who was accompanied by his future wife.

In December 2004, The Chief of the General Staff, General Sir Mike Jackson, announced changes the structure of the infantry. The rationale behind the changes is based on the operational need for more agile, deployable and flexible force. Single battalion regiments will move towards a larger regimental structure consisting of two or more battalions and same time the number of individual infantry battalions would be reduced by four. Following discussions between the Colonels of Regiments within the Prince of Wales's Division, it was announced that the 1st Battalion The Royal Regiment of Wales (24th/41st Foot) would form the 2nd Battalion of a new, larger regiment with the title 'The Royal Welsh'. The change would take effect on 1st March 2006.

Section 10

AUXILIARY, RESERVE AND CADET FORCES

The Militia
1757–1920

The Militia, sometimes referred to as the Constitutional Force, is the oldest of Britain's auxiliary forces and has an ancestry rooted in the military obligations of the Anglo-Saxons. These obligations were transmitted through medieval legislation to be enshrined in the first militia statutes of 1558. Thereafter, the Militia had a formal statutory existence almost continuously until 1908. Service was mostly based on property and wealth but, from 1757, manpower was raised by compulsory ballot and, after 1852, by voluntary enlistment. The militia regiments of the respective counties were, in 1757, reorganised as infantry regiments, under the control of the Lords Lieutenant, whose members were obliged to train annually and were required to render continuous service when their regiments were embodied for home garrison duties in time of war.

Thus the county militia regiments in Wales were embodied for service during the Seven Years' War, the American War of Independence, the French Revolutionary Wars and between 1803 and 1816 for the long embodiment of the Napoleonic period when, in addition to their services in the home garrisons and Ireland, they provided hundreds of trained men for service with the regular army, and thus contributed to the success of British units abroad. In recognition of their contribution during the Napoleonic period, each of the Welsh county Militia battalions was given the appellation 'Royal'. A period of decline from 1817 to 1851 ended in 1852 with a revival of the militia nationally, and in 1881 the Cardwell Reforms brought the militia under the control of the War Office and closer to their 'territorial' regular battalions.

In North Wales, the 1881 Reforms saw the creation of the 3rd and 4th Battalions of the Royal Welsh Fusiliers, with their titles finally being established in 1890 as the 3rd Battalion The Royal Welsh Fusiliers (Royal Denbigh and Flint Militia) and 4th Battalion The Royal Welsh Fusiliers (Royal

Carnarvon and Merioneth Militia) – the Anglesey Militia having become Engineers in 1877. In 1908, the 4th Battalion was disbanded and the 3rd became a Special Reserve battalion. During the Great War, it acted as a Depot, first in Wrexham and then Liverpool, before being sent in November 1917 to Limerick because of fears of possible *Sinn Fein* activity. It was disembodied in 1919.

In South Wales in 1876, the militia quotas of Radnor and Brecon were united under the title The Royal South Wales Borderers Militia (Royal Radnor and Brecknock Rifles). Five years later, the Royal South Wales Borderers Militia and the Royal Montgomery Rifles Militia were respectively re-designated as the 3rd and 4th (Militia) Battalions, The South Wales Borderers. The Royal Glamorgan Light Infantry Militia became the 3rd (Militia) Battalion, The Welsh Regiment. [The Royal Monmouthshire Militia had become Engineers in 1877 and exist today as the Royal Monmouthshire Royal Engineers (Militia)]. The 3rd South Wales Borderers and 3rd Welsh volunteered to serve overseas and were involved in lines of communication duties during the Second Boer War. In 1908, the 4th South Wales Borderers was disbanded and the remaining two militia battalions became Special Reserve battalions of their respective regiments and as such provided the active service battalions of the regiments with a steady flow of reinforcements throughout the Great War. The two battalions stood down in 1920 and, although officially listed until 1953, were never again reactivated.

The Volunteers 1858–1908

The Volunteers, which had existed at various times simultaneously with the Militia, are principally associated with the Napoleonic period, 1794–1816, as volunteer infantry and mounted yeomanry. The hostile attitude adopted by France in the late 1850s forced the British government in 1859 to authorise the raising of a permanent part-time volunteer force. To begin with, these county rifle volunteer corps were largely independent, choosing their own style of uniform and administering themselves at very little cost to the public. The reforms instituted by Cardwell in the period 1868–74 aimed to weld the Regular, Militia and Volunteers into one homogeneous army. In 1873, the country was divided into regimental districts, each with a depot for Regular battalions; the Militia and Volunteer units in the district were then linked to the local Regulars. This re-organisation was carried a stage further in 1881, when Volunteer units adopted the same territorial titles as their constituent regular unit.

In North Wales, with a Regimental District (or Depot) at Wrexham, the 1st Denbighshire and the 1st Flintshire and Carnarvonshire Rifle Volunteer Corps were affiliated to the Royal Welsh Fusiliers and in 1884 became the 1st and 2nd (Volunteer) Battalions, The Royal Welsh Fusiliers respectively. Thirteen years later, a 3rd (Volunteer) Battalion was formed as an offshoot of 2nd.

The rifle volunteer corps of Brecon, Monmouth and Radnor became the 1st (Brecknockshire) Volunteer Battalion and those in Monmouthshire the 2nd, 3rd and 4th Volunteer Battalions, The South Wales Borderers with a Regimental District (or Depot) being established at Brecon. In 1897, a further battalion called the 5th (Volunteer) Battalion The South Wales Borderers was raised in Montgomery and Cardiganshire.

In South and West Wales, the rifle volunteer corps of Pembrokeshire and Glamorgan became the 1st, 2nd and 3rd (Volunteer) Battalions, The Welsh Regiment with a Regimental District (or Depot) based in Cardiff. The 3rd Glamorgan Rifle Volunteers (whose Colonel was then HRH The Prince of Wales) which was nominally 4th Volunteer Battalion, retained its old title.

The first overseas service for Volunteer units came in 1900 when they provided composite active service companies to serve, with their Regular counterparts, 1st Battalion The Royal Welsh Fusiliers, 2nd Battalion The South Wales Borderers and 1st Battalion The Welsh Regiment, against the Boers in South Africa, thus gaining the first battle honour 'South Africa 1900–02' for their respective Volunteer battalions.

Territorial Force
1908–20

In 1908, when the Territorial Force (TF) was formed, the three Volunteer battalions of the Royal Welsh Fusiliers became the 4th, 5th and 6th Battalions The Royal Welsh Fusiliers, and the 5th (Volunteer) Battalion The South Wales Borderers, based in Montgomeryshire, became the 7th Battalion. In the following year, their official titles became the 4th (Denbighshire), 5th (Flintshire), 6th (Carnarvonshire and Anglesey) and 7th (Merioneth and Montgomery) Battalions, The Royal Welsh Fusiliers (TF). The remaining four volunteer battalions of the South Wales Borderers became the Brecknockshire Battalion, The South Wales Borderers; 1st, 2nd and 3rd Battalions, The Monmouthshire Regiment. The 1st Monmouths, fiercely maintaining their rifle antecedence, retained their dark-green rifle uniforms with black buttons. The 1st and 3rd Volunteer Battalions of The Welsh Regiment became the 4th and 5th Battalions. The 2nd Volunteer Battalion converted to Artillery. The 3rd Glamorgan Rifle Volunteers formed the 6th Battalion, The Welsh Regiment (TF). A new battalion, to be called 7th (Cyclist) Battalion The Welsh Regiment (TF), was authorised.

All first-line battalions fought with great distinction in the Great War, the 4th Battalion The Royal Welsh Fusiliers, the three battalions of the Monmouthshire Regiment and 6th Battalion The Welsh Regiment saw service in France and Flanders, and the rest with the 53rd (Welsh) Division in Gallipoli, Egypt and Palestine. The 2nd Monmouths had the distinction of being the first Territorial unit to be allocated a battalion sector in the trenches in December 1914. At the end of the war they were the only British Territorial battalion to march into Germany.

The Brecknockshire Battalion saw active service in Aden in 1915, gaining a Battle Honour, before becoming a garrison battalion in India. The 7th Battalion, The Welsh Regiment remained in Britain as a garrison battalion.

Three new Territorial battalions were formed in Egypt in 1917 when five dismounted Welsh Yeomanry regiments: the Denbighshire Yeomanry; Glamorgan Yeomanry; Pembroke Yeomanry; Welsh Horse and Montgomeryshire Yeomanry were converted to infantry to form the 24th (Denbighshire Yeomanry) and 25th (Montgomery and Welsh Horse Yeomanry) Battalions The Royal Welsh Fusiliers and the 24th (Pembroke and Glamorgan Yeomanry) Battalion The Welsh Regiment. They were soon engaged in Egypt, Palestine and Syria. At Beersheba in October 1917, Corporal Collins of the 25th Battalion The Royal Welsh Fusiliers gained a Victoria Cross for bringing in wounded under heavy fire and saving many lives. This battalion was awarded its second Victoria Cross in September 1918 when Sergeant Waring was killed when leading a successful attack against four enemy machine guns at Ronssoy in France.

Territorial Army

Inter-War Years, 1921–39

After the Great War, all Territorial Force battalions were disbanded but were soon re-activated in 1921 with the formation of the new Territorial Army (TA). The four pre-war Royal Welch Fusiliers battalions continued as before. The 7th Welch was amalgamated with the 6th Battalion, thus leaving the Welch Regiment with three Territorial Battalions viz: 4th Carmarthenshire Battalion, and the 5th and 6th Glamorganshire Battalions. The Brecknocks were absorbed by the 3rd Monmouths.

Further changes occurred in 1938 when, with the increasing threat to mainland Britain, the 5th Battalion The Royal Welch Fusiliers, became an anti-tank unit with the Royal Artillery; the 1st Monmouths and 6th Welch were converted into searchlight regiments and they too were lost to the Royal Artillery.

Finally, in 1939, shortly before the outbreak of war, the strength of the TA was doubled and the following new battalions were formed: the 8th, 9th and 10th The Royal Welch Fusiliers (out of the 4th, 6th and 7th Battalions respectively); the 4th Monmouths (out of 2nd Monmouths); the Brecknocks (out of 3rd Monmouths); the 15th Welch (out of 4th Welch) and the 2/5th Welch (out of 5th Welch).

Second World War, 1939–45

The Territorial battalions were embodied in 1939. The 4th, 6th and 7th Battalions The Royal Welch Fusiliers; the 2nd Monmouths and the 4th and 1/5th Battalions Welch were to serve with the 53rd (Welsh) Division in the United Kingdom until June 1944. Shortly after D-Day, the division moved to reinforce the Normandy bridgehead and thereafter, through to VE Day, th battalions were actively involved in the liberation of France, the Low Countries and the advance into Northern Germany. Also involved in the fight through North West Europe were the 3rd Monmouths, serving as part of 11th Armoured Division; in ten months the battalion's casualties amounted to over 1,100 (including 67 officers) of which 267 (including two commanding officers) were killed. Two Victoria Crosses were awarded to TA soldiers during the North West Europe campaign (1944–5). The first was gained by Lieutenant Tasker Watkins of 1/5th Battalion, The Welch Regiment, near Barfour during the fighting for Falaise in Normandy in August 1944. The other was awarded to Corporal Edward Chapman of 3rd Monmouths during fighting in the wooded Teutoburger Wald in Germany in April 1945. After the war, Corporal Chapman was to continue to serve as a senior NCO with the 2nd Monmouths.

At this time the 8th, 9th and 10th Battalions, The Royal Welch Fusiliers; the Brecknocks and the 2/5th and 15th Welch served in the United Kingdom in home defence, training and draft finding roles, and provided between them many hundreds of trained soldiers for active service with the first line and Regular battalions of the regiment. In 1942, the 10th Battalion, The Royal Welch Fusiliers was converted to a parachute role, for which over two-thirds of its members volunteered, and was renamed 6th (Royal Welch) Parachute Battalion.

Post-Second World War, 1945–67

Just after the war, in 1946, all TA battalions were disbanded but the following year the TA was reactivated and the 4th, 6th and 7th Battalions, The Royal Welch Fusiliers; 2nd and 3rd Monmouths and 4th and 5th Welch were re-formed. By 1947, the former 6th and 7th Battalions Royal Welch Fusiliers and 3rd Monmouths had been converted to light anti-aircraft regiments with the Royal Artillery. In 1956, a 6th/7th Royal Welch Fusiliers was formed with its headquarters in Caernarfon and 6th Welch re-appeared, being re-formed from 16th (Welsh) Parachute Battalion (TA).

Territorial & Auxiliary Volunteer Reserve (T&AVR)

1967–71

In 1967, the TA was drastically reduced in size and re-named the Territorial & Auxiliary Volunteer Reserve (T&AVR). A single infantry battalion, called The Welsh Volunteers, comprising companies from each of the three Welsh infantry regiments, was raised in Wales with a NATO support role, while the existing TA battalions (retaining the title Territorial) were given a purely home-defence role and reduced to cadre form.

1971–99

In April 1971, an expansion of the volunteers occurred. The Welsh Volunteers

Battalion was replaced by the 3rd (Volunteer) Battalion, The Royal Welch Fusiliers and the 3rd and 4th (Volunteer) Battalions, The Royal Regiment of Wales which absorbed the existing T&AVR companies and the cadres of the Territorial battalions. The Headquarters of those battalions were based on Wrexham, Cardiff and Llanelli respectively. In April 1985, each battalion was augmented by a Home Service Force (HSF) company, comprising of volunteers who wished a reduced training commitment. These HSF companies had a short life and were disbanded in March 1993. In April 1986, the battalions were again augmented, gaining an extra rifle company. The headquarters of 4th Battalion, The Royal Regiment of Wales, moved from Llanelli in 1987, when a new TA Centre, named after Sir Tasker Watkins VC, was opened at Morfa in Swansea. In October 1993, in yet another re-organisation, this time a reduction, 3rd and 4th Battalions, The Royal Regiment of Wales, merged to form the 2nd (Volunteer) Battalion, The Royal Regiment of Wales.

Territorial Army

1999–to date

Further reductions to the TA were implemented in July 1999 when the 3rd (Volunteer) Battalion, The Royal Welch Fusiliers amalgamated with 2nd (Volunteer) Battalion, The Royal Regiment of Wales to form a new volunteer regiment, The Royal Welsh Regiment (RWR). Two rifle companies (Wrexham and Caernarfon) were badged RWF, with Headquarters (Cardiff) and two rifle companies (Swansea and Pontypridd) badged RRW. The battalion hosted and administered the Territorial Army Band of Wales (The Royal Regiment of Wales) based in Newport, Monmouthshire which took part in many public and military events across the Principality.

The Royal Welsh Regiment continued to provide an increasing number of individual TA soldiers for six-month operational tours of duty working alongside their Regular counterparts in the Balkans, Afghanistan and Iraq. In March 2006, this battalion became part of the new 'Royal Welsh' family, being designated 3rd Battalion, The Royal Welsh.

Home Guard

Other elements of the antecedent regiments of The Royal Welsh were 'Volunteer' battalions whose soldiers wore regimental cap badges raised in Wales during the Great War – these units were the forerunners of the more well-known county Home Guard units of the Second World War, who also wore their antecedent regiment's cap badge. Worthy of special mention is Private G Jones of the Monmouthshire Home Guard who was awarded a Military Medal for rescuing a seriously wounded comrade during a heavy German air-raid on Newport Docks in July 1940; thought to be the only incident of this gallantry medal being awarded for an action on the mainland of Britain.

Cadets

The Army Cadet Force, which continues to provide a challenging youth organisation for boys and girls and a source of recruits for the Regular and Reserve forces, has county based battalions in Wales. In many towns and small communities, these isolated Cadet detachments are the only representatives of the army in the locality and many of these cadets now wear the cap badge of The Royal Welsh. Those in the pre-1997 counties of Clwyd, Glamorgan and Gwynedd immediately strengthened their links with the regiment by formally adopting the subsidiary titles of 4th (Cadet) Battalion, 5th (Cadet) Battalion and 6th (Cadet) Battalion of The Royal Welsh respectively. Subsequently, a further re-organisation of the ACF took place in April 2009 which linked together the pre-1997 counties of Clwyd and Gwynedd, Dyfed and Glamorgan, and Gwent and Powys, and the regimental battalion titles were dropped.

The Royal Welsh also has connections with schools that have Combined Cadet Force units, including Monmouth School, Christ College (Brecon), Llandovery College, Ruthin School, St Bridget's School (Denbigh) and Hartridge High School (Newport). Monmouth School CCF is the only unit that continues to wear the Monmouthshire Regiment cap badge.

Section 11

THE NEW REGIMENT – THE ROYAL WELSH 2006

Regular Army

1st Battalion, The Royal Welsh (The Royal Welch Fusiliers)
The 1st Battalion, The Royal Welsh, following the Formation Parade, moved from their base in Mons Barracks, Aldershot to the Sovereign Base Area in Cyprus where it had the 'Light Role'. During the battalion's two-year deployment in Cyprus, besides guarding key installations on the island and providing, at short notice, a reserve for Iraq, it undertook two four-month deployments to the Falkland Islands and took part in a challenging exercise in Jordan. In 2007, Battalion Headquarters and two companies were deployed from Cyprus to Afghanistan on Operation HERRICK and third company to Iraq on Op TELIC. One fusilier later received the MC and NATOs Meritorious Service Medal for his action in Afghanistan. The battalion returned to a permanent base at The Dale Barracks, Chester in August 2008.

In 2009, the 1st Battalion were warned for deployment on Op HERRICK 11 in Afghanistan. However, the political environment prevailing at the time meant that the battalion's departure date and role was unclear. Nevertheless the battalion weathered the uncertainty and deployed in good spirits on 4th December 2009. In the first part of the deployment the battalion was involved in the United States led Op MOSHTARAK, the largest aviation assault for a number of years involving soldiers from a number of countries making up the Royal Welsh Battle Group. Later, the 1st Battalion participated in security operations in Nad-e Ali and western Babjaji districts (known as Area 31). The battalion returned home on 4th May 2010 having suffered one fatality. In the subsequent operational awards the battalion was honoured with one OBE, two MCs, three Mentioned in Despatches and six Joint Commander's Commendations.

2nd Battalion The Royal Welsh (The Royal Regiment of Wales)
The 2nd Battalion, The Royal Welsh are based in Lucknow Barracks in Tidworth, Wiltshire. The barracks provide one-man, en-suite rooms for 600 soldiers. For operational purposes, the battalion forms part of 1st Mechanised Brigade and is equipped with Warrior armoured personnel-carriers. In May 2007, the battalion returned to Basra on Operation TELIC, its third deployment to that theatre. The battalion suffered over 50 casualties during the six-month tour, including three fatalities (as well as two further fatalities amongst soldiers attached from 3 R SCOTS). The battalion returned to the UK in later November 2007 and received a tumultuous welcome home in December both in Cardiff Castle and the Millennium Stadium. Thousands of people turned out on a particularly cold day to witness the battalion march through the streets of the City of Cardiff. Campaign medals were presented by the Adjutant General, Lieutenant-General Sir Frederick Viggers and Major-General Andrew Farquhar (GOC 5 Division). The operational awards published in 2008 contained one OBE, two MCs, nine Mentioned in Despatches, one Queen's Commendation for Valuable Service (QCVS) and a further seven members of the 2nd Battalion received Joint Commander's Commendations. The QCVS was awarded to a Territorial soldier on attachment from 3rd Battalion, The Royal Welsh.

Over the next two years, the 2nd Battalion provided eighteen months of continuous Armoured Infantry (AI) support in Afghanistan; C Company Group on Op HERRICK 10, A Company on Op HERRICK 11 and B (Rorke's Drift) Company on Op HERRICK 13; with a number of individual officers and soldiers from the battalion attached 16th Air Assault Brigade on Op HERRICK 13.

Territorial Army

3rd Battalion, The Royal Welsh TA
The 3rd Battalion, The Royal Welsh is the only Territorial Army infantry unit that recruits from the whole of Wales. Previously, the battalion was known as The Royal Welsh Regiment which had been formed on 1st July 1999 when the 3rd (Volunteer) Battalion, The Royal Welch Fusiliers and the 2nd (Volunteer) Battalion, The Royal Regiment of Wales were amalgamated at Otterburn

Camp, Northumberland. With its headquarters in Maindy Barracks Cardiff, the 3rd Battalion has sub-units in Aberystwyth, Caernarfon, Colwyn Bay, Newport, Queensferry, Pontypridd, Swansea and Wrexham. A number of officers and soldiers of the 3rd Battalion have recently served on operational tours in Bosnia, Iraq and Afghanistan.

The Regimental Band of The Royal Welsh

The Regimental Band of The Royal Welsh has versatility of style and repertoire, which is both unique and highly popular, whether on parade as a marching band or on the concert platform. Their playing, marching and singing portrays that musical quality for which the band is renowned throughout Wales. It is also interesting to note that the band is the last surviving all-brass band left within the British Army and all its musicians are members of the Territorial Army.

The Band have travelled abroad extensively, including countries such as Belgium, Germany, Canada, France, Australia and, in 2009, toured Nova Scotia. The band also plays at many major sporting events, in particular at international rugby matches featuring the Wales team where its continuing presence at the world-famous Millennium Stadium in Cardiff has been greatly appreciated by rugby spectators across the world. On many of the outside engagements, the band is enhanced by the presence of the Corps of Drums of the 3rd Battalion, The Royal Welsh which, in its own inimitable style and expertise, always adds the final polish to any engagement.

Section 12

BADGES, DRESS AND DISTINCTIONS

The uniforms worn by officers and soldiers in The Royal Welsh reflect a significant part of the history of their former antecedent regiments. Over time, doubtless The Royal Welsh will develop its own distinctive customs and traditions, and those it has inherited will evolve; but history reflected in the regiment's dress and accoutrements provides modern soldiers with a tangible link with the past, and is a source of pride and individuality to its people and an essential element of esprit de corps.

BADGES

The Badge of the Heir Apparent (The Three Plumes)
The Regimental Cap Badge
This regimental badge or device was granted to the 23rd Foot in 1714 on the change of title of the regiment to The Prince of Wales's Own Royal Regiment of Welsh Fuzileers, in recognition of its service in Marlborough's campaigns. It is possible that this badge could have been used by the regiment earlier than 1714. It appeared on the Colours in 1742 and its use was confirmed by Royal Warrant, dated 1st July 1751. It consists of three white feathers (or plumes) behind a gold coronet. The scroll below the coronet bears the motto *Ich Dien* (German for 'I Serve').

For the 41st Foot, the use of the Prince of Wales's Plumes was authorised in December 1831 and the badge appeared as a device, together with the regimental motto, on the Colours that were presented to the regiment in 1841. These Colours were carried throughout the subsequent Afghan campaign. In 1881, the Plumes were adopted as the centre badge of the helmet plate of the Welsh Regiment and later, in 1899, were adopted as the cap badge on the introduction of service-dress caps. This cap badge, with the scroll 'THE

WELSH' and later 'THE WELCH' beneath, was worn with distinction by thousands of Welshmen throughout the two World Wars.

A simplified version of this badge was introduced in 1960 as a common badge to be worn by all three infantry regiments in the Welsh Brigade and the familiar regimental cap badges worn by Welsh soldiers since before the Great War were discontinued. However, in 1970, the Royal Welch Fusiliers reverted to their previous badge, a grenade flamed, proper, inscribed 'Royal Welch Fusiliers', within the crest of The Prince of Wales.

On its formation in 1969, soldiers of The Royal Regiment of Wales continued to wear the Welsh Brigade simplified design despite disapproval by many as it did not conform to the traditional design for The Prince of Wales's crest. Accordingly, in 1973, steps were taken to rectify this and a number of draft sketches were prepared and rejected, before one was finally accepted by the Regimental Committee and approved by the Colonel-in-Chief, the Prince of Wales. This design was submitted to the College of Arms and the Army Dress Committee. In the event, its approval was a formality and a revised design was introduced for the Royal Regiment of Wales in November 1975. It is this 1975 badge, slightly smaller in size, differenced by a scroll with the words 'THE ROYAL WELSH', which became the current cap badge is based. Soldiers wear a silver anodised version with a green square backing. Officers and Warrant Officers wear an embroidered version, with the edging in green integral to the badge when used with a beret, and blue edged when worn with the No. 1 dress cap. A larger version of the cap badge is used in the front of bearskin and seal-skin caps and on the front of pioneers' aprons when in ceremonial dress.

This crest is thought to have originated with Edward, the Black Prince, eldest son of Edward III. According to legend, the Black Prince obtained the arms from John of Bohemia, against whom he fought in the battle of Crécy in 1346. After the battle, the prince went over to the body of the dead king (whom he admired for his bravery) and took his helmet, lined with ostrich feathers. The feathers and the dead king's motto made up the prince's new badge and came to be used by subsequent Princes of Wales. Technically, the badge should be described as the Duke of Cornwall's plumes or feathers, as the badge is that of the eldest son of the sovereign, whether or not he has been invested as Prince of Wales.

This badge, without the scroll 'THE ROYAL WELSH' and with a red background, appears as the centre badge on both the Sovereign's and the Regimental Colours of the Royal Welsh. This special distinction follows the tradition established in 1747 when thirteen regiments were specifically authorised to bear centre badges on both Colours. The thirteen included both the 23rd Foot and the 41st Foot.

The Regimental Crest

The Regimental Crest of The Royal Welsh consists of the badges and distinctions taken from the antecedent regiments. It is a red dragon rampant within a wreath of immortelles (qv), with the Regimental Motto (qv) *Gwell Angau Na Chywilydd*, surmounted by the Crown. This crest will form the centre badge on the drums, the colour belts and other accoutrements.

The Royal Cypher

In addition to the rose and thistle within the garter (the badge of the Royal Hospital Chelsea), the 41st Regiment, or The Invalids, used the King's Cypher and Crown from the time of the Royal Warrant of 1751. The Royal Regiment of Wales, and now The Royal Welsh, continued with this tradition. The Royal Cypher appears in first quarter of the Regimental Colour.

The Red Dragon

The red dragon badge, like the Prince of Wales's plumes, was granted to the 23rd Foot in 1714 on the change of title of the regiment to The Prince of Wales's Own Royal Regiment of Welsh Fuzileers, in recognition of its service in Marlborough's campaigns. It appeared on the 1742 Regimental Colour and its use was confirmed by Royal Warrant dated 1st July 1751 when it was described as one of the devices of Edward, the Black Prince. The design is a dragon rampant and remained remarkably unchanged through nearly 300 years. In 1881, the dragon, in a passant style, was authorised to be used as their principal badge by all Welsh infantry regiments, but in the event was only used by the South Wales Borderers (and later by the Monmouthshire Regiment). However, the red dragon passant, surrounded by the wreath of immortelles, was approved as the centre badge on the Regimental Colour of The Royal Regiment of Wales. The dragon rampant is therefore a badge of significance as it forms the centre of the Regimental Crest (qv) of The Royal Welsh. It also appears in the second quarter on the Regimental Colour, and on the collar badges and regimental buttons.

The White Horse of Hanover

This device was awarded to 23rd Foot, but its adoption by the regiment is uncertain. Before 1807, there were three badges (or devices) in the corners of the Regimental Colour of the 23rd, viz: the rising sun, the plumes (with the motto *ICH DIEN*) and the Red Dragon. The White Horse of Hanover replaced the corner badge of the Plumes in 1807. This, together with the motto *NEC ASPERA TERRENT*, was not authorised officially for the 23rd Foot until the Royal Warrant of 1835. The confusion about the adoption of the White Horse of Hanover appears to have arisen because it was authorised as the badge for the mitre caps for all infantry Grenadier companies in the 1751 Warrant. There are illustrations of soldiers of both 23rd and 24th Foot wearing the White Horse on their caps. The motto translates as 'Neither do difficulties deter us' or, as is more commonly quoted, 'Difficulties be Damned'. The White Horse appears in third quarter of the Regimental Colour of The Royal Welsh.

The Rising Sun

The Rising Sun was also the badge of Edward, the Black Prince and was granted to the 23rd Foot in 1714. It appeared on the 1742 Regimental Colour and its use was confirmed by the Royal Warrant of July 1751. The Rising Sun appears in the fourth quarter of the Regimental Colour of The Royal Welsh.

A Naval Crown superscribed '12TH APRIL 1782' subscribed 'ST VINCENT 1797'

The Naval Crown commemorates the 69th Regiment's action as marines at the battle of the Saints in 1782. In October 1951, the Welch Regiment was permitted to associate the Battle Honour 'ST VINCENT, 14TH FEBRUARY 1797' with the Naval Crown. The Royal Welsh thus inherits these two naval honours. The Naval Crown appears at the bottom the Battle Honour wreath on the Regimental Colour of The Royal Welsh.

The Sphinx superscribed 'EGYPT'

The Sphinx commemorates the participation of the 23rd and 24th Regiments in the Battle of Alexandria in July 1801 (authorised in 1802). The Sphinx on the Colour represents a Battle Honour, even though it does not have a separate Battle Honour scroll. Beneath the Sphinx are 'the Laurels', again awarded to both regiments after their participation in the Peninsular campaign (1808_14). The Sphinx with the Laurels appears at the base of the Regimental Colour of the Royal Welsh.

Collar Badges

There are four versions of collar badges worn by The Royal Welsh. The badge is a grenade 'flamed proper', with a dragon passant within a Wreath of Immortelles (qv) in silver gilt on the ball. All are of similar size. The position of the dragon depends on the type of collar and ensures that the dragon always faces inwards. (1) Soldiers' collar badges in anodised gold gilt for No. 2 dress (2) Officers' collar badges in gunmetal for service dress (3) Soldiers' collar badges in anodised gold gilt for No. 1 dress (4) Officers' collar badges in embroidered gold for No. 1 dress, and full dress for officers, warrant officers and drum major, and for officers, warrant officers' and sergeants' mess dress.

Company Colours and Badges

In addition to Regimental, or Battalion, Colours, up until the mid-18th century, each infantry regiment had company, or maker, colours used to indicate company lines in tented camps. The colours were carried by the senior sergeant in each company, i.e. the 'colour' sergeant. Likewise, the commanding officer and adjutant would have their own marker colours placed at the entrance to their respective tents. These company colours have now disappeared except in the Foot Guards, the Honourable Artillery Company and 1st Battalion The Royal Welsh. The badges or devices used on these colours within the 1st Battalion are by tradition are as follows (background colour shown in brackets): A Company, The Rising Sun (green); B Company, The Crest of the Prince of Wales (orange); C Company, The White Horse of Hanover (red); D Company, The Sphinx (yellow); Support Company, The Minden Rose (red and white); and Headquarter Company, The Red Dragon (royal blue).

Battalion Camp Flags

The design of camp flags and battalion signboards consist of a red dragon passant on a field of blue and green, surrounded by a blue border with the regiment's name in both English and Welsh.

Dress

Headdress

Order of Dress	*Wearer*	*Form of Headdress*
Full Dress	Officers, Director of Music (or Bandmaster), Warrant Officers, Drum Major	Bearskin caps with large Royal Welsh cap badge in front and white plume on the right
	Goat Major	Foreign Service (white) helmet with spike, chin-chain, Royal Welsh helmet plate (no backing cloth) in front
	Musicians, Drummers, Pioneers, Escort to the Colours	Seal-skin caps with large Royal Welsh cap badge in front and white plume on the right
No. 1 Dress	Officers and Warrant Officers	Forage Cap, with red piping and band and embroidered Royal Welsh cap badge
	Soldiers	Dark blue beret with white plume with silver anodised Royal Welsh cap badge with a green square backing
No. 2 Dress	Officers and Warrant Officers	Forage Cap, with red piping and band and embroidered Royal Welsh cap badge (plain 3/4 inch gold embroidered peak for field officers)

	Officers and Warrant Officers Class 1	Khaki Service Dress Cap with bronzed Royal Welsh cap badge
	Soldiers	Khaki beret with anodised Royal Welsh cap badge with a green square backing and white plume
No. 8 Dress (combat)	Officers and Warrant Officers	Khaki beret with embroidered Royal Welsh cap badge
	Soldiers	Khaki beret with anodised Royal Welsh cap badge with a green square backing and white plume

Bearskin Caps

A black bearskin cap was first authorised for the 23rd Foot in 1768. It was 12 inches high, exclusive of fur, and fitted with a black japanned metal plate with, in white metal, the lion of England standing on a helmet, with a 'G' on one side and an 'R' on the other. On the back of the cap was a red cloth circle with Prince of Wales's feathers in white (silver for officers), below which was a grenade and the regimental number.

In about 1802, a new pattern cap was authorised to be worn by Fusiliers and the grenadier companies of other regiments. The cap had a leather peak, brass front plate, white cords and tassels (gold for officers) on the right side, and a white plume on the left. Minor changes occurred until the peak and brass plate were abolished in 1835.

The bearskin cap was abolished for all ranks in 1844, except for those in the Foot Guards. Four years later, however, the uniform of the Regimental Band of the 23rd Foot is described as consisting of 'a bearskin cap, with gilt grenade in front and a gilt chin-chain'. In 1865, the shako was replaced by a short lambskin cap, which, in 1867, was superseded, first by black sealskin and then by otter skin, with a white plume on the left-hand side. In 1871, the white plume was discontinued and seal-skin replaced otter.

In 1900, the height of the cap was varied according to that of the wearer and the skin used was either bear or black seal. Embellishments included the regimental badge, a gilt burnished chin-chain, black velvet and leather lining, and a white 6$^{1}/_{2}$-inch feather on the right side with a gilt flame socket. This pattern remained in force until the abolition of full dress uniform. Ceremonial pioneers, musicians and drummers have continued to wear the shorter sealskin caps to this day. Officers, the Director of Music, warrant officers and the Drum Major wear full-sized bearskin caps with a cut white feather plume when in full dress.

The White Plume

The custom of wearing the white hackle (or more correctly 'a plume') originated in 1702 when the 23rd Foot was formed into a regiment of fusiliers and a grenadier company style head-dress was introduced throughout the regiment. Around 1709, officers began to adopt the wearing of feathers in their hats, and this was officially sanctioned in 1789 when the colour of the hackle was laid down as white. The custom was continued with varying types of head-dress up to and including the bearskin and racoon-skin caps, and the topee worn with tropical kit. It was not, however, considered suitable for wear with either the flat khaki service-dress cap or with other khaki head gear which followed. After the introduction of the blue beret, it was authorised in 1950 as a distinction in fusilier regiments. It is worn by non commissioned officers and soldiers of The Royal Welsh when in No. 1 dress (blue beret) and with a khaki beret when in No. 2 dress and in combat/training dress. The hackle is not worn when soldiers are wearing Gore-Tex or camouflage cream, nor it is worn by officers and warrant officers when in No. 1, No. 2 or No. 8 (combat) dress.

The Flash

In the days when soldiers had pigtails they were worn powdered and greased. In order to protect their jackets, soldiers enclosed the pigtails in what was known as a 'queue bag'. In 1808, hair was ordered to be cut close to the neck and the queue was abolished. The officers of the Royal Welch Fusiliers decided to retain the ribbons with which the queue was tied, and, using an old slang term for a wig, they were known as the 'Flash'. In 1834, when the 23rd Foot arrived in England after over ten years in Gibraltar, an inspecting general complained about the 'superfluous decoration on the collar of the coat' and the matter was referred to the King. King William IV was pleased to approve the Flash 'as a peculiarity whereby to mark the dress of that distinguished regiment'. Until 1900 it was worn only by the officers, warrant officers and colour sergeants of the Royal Welch Fusiliers, but in that year its use was extended to all ranks when in full dress. In 1924, it was approved for wear on ceremonial parades and when walking out. Today, the Flash is worn by all who are 'badged' The Royal Welsh, including regular, territorial and cadet battalions. It is worn at the back, sewn inside the collar, in full dress, N°. 1 and N°. 2 dress, and consists of five black ribbons; the soldier's flash is 153mm (6 ins) long and that for officers and warrant officers is 230mm (9 ins) inches long.

Officers' rank badges – The Eversleigh Star

From about 1890, the officers of the South Wales Borderers took to wearing a unique and distinctive pattern of 'Eversleigh' Star and large (Edward) Crown as their badges of rank. These remained unique until 1928 when The Middlesex Regiment (now The Princess of Wales's Royal Regiment) adopted a similar design. The origin is obscure, but the regiment continued to wear them, quite unofficially, until 1956 when they became formally authorised; but it was not until 1988 that they became a free issue. Today, the officers of The Royal Welsh wear large Edward Crown (with a crimson cushion) and Eversleigh Star rank badges when in N°. 1 dress and in bronze (gun-metal) when in khaki N°. 2 service dress. [Note it is pronounced 'Everleigh']. In combat dress, olive slides with black stars and crowns with insignia 'R WELSH' are worn.

Warrant and Non-Commissioned Officers' Rank Badges

The wearing of rank badges, with edging in green on both arms, adopted by the South Wales Borderers in the late 1960s, is continued in The Royal Welsh when wearing N°. 2 dress. This distinction is unique in the infantry. In full dress and N°. 1 dress traditional line infantry rank badges are worn only on the right arm and are edged in red. In combat dress, slides in disrupted pattern material (DPM) with olive/brown rank and insignia 'R WELSH' are worn.

Collar Badges and Buttons

The collar badge of The Royal Welsh is a flaming grenade with a dragon passant within a wreath of immortelles mounted on the ball of grenade. These are worn in woven silver for officer's mess dress, bronze (gun-metal) finish in service dress (to match bronze rank badges), gilt finish for No. 1 dress and anodised for soldiers. The dragon rampant inscribed 'THE ROYAL WELSH' is used as the device on regimental buttons. Buttons are bronze finish for officers' service dress, gilt finish for No. 1 dress and anodised for soldiers.

Tactical Recognition Flashes

At the time of formation soldiers of each battalion of The Royal Welsh continued to wear tactical recognition flashes (TRF) on the combat/training dress of their former regiments; viz: 1st Battalion – red dragon rampant on blue background; 2nd Battalion – red dragon passant on green background; and 3rd Battalion – blue and green horizontal stripes.

Belts

The colours of the regimental stable belt, worn with combat/training dress, are the adopted regimental colours and are subdued hues of the colours of the former Welsh Brigade. Its description is as follows: blue (navy, top 30mm), red (scarlet, middle 4mm) and green (Wimbledon, bottom 30mm), with black leather two strap buckle worn on the left side. For full dress, a white metal regimental buckle, for use with white buff equipment, is decorated with a Wreath of Immortelles on the female clasp and the Prince of Wales's plumes or feathers on the male clasp, all in anodised white metal.

Regimental Mess Dress (No. 10 dress)

Officers: Prince of Wales's Division pattern high collar scarlet mess jacket, blue cuffs and collar, with embroidered grenade collar badges, and regimental flash at the back of the jacket, shoulder straps with embroidered rank badges with a green mess vest fastened at the side, with gold braid piping round the top, down the front and along the bottom seams, and blue overall trousers with 1/4 inch red stripe down side seams.

Senior Ranks: Plain red open collar mess jacket, worn with white shirt and black bowtie, with embroidered grenade collar badges, and regimental flash at the back of the jacket, with a green Mess

Waistcoat fastened with four buttons, and No. 1 dress trousers with one inch red stripe down side seams. Rank badges worn on right arm.

Distinctions

A Royal Regiment

Since the creation of 'Our Guards and Garrisons' by King Charles II in 1661, it had become the practice to confer a Royal title on selected regiments as a mark of long and distinguished service or, in more recent times, for gallantry in action. The 23rd (The Royal Welch Fusiliers) was one of the earliest regiments to be granted this appellation, receiving it in 1712. It is a privilege, but the honour confers neither precedence nor seniority. All Royal regiments were, and are distinguished, by royal-blue facings, but since 1935 regiments awarded the honour have been granted permission, at their request, to retain their original facings. The Royal Welsh therefore continues the tradition of The Royal Welch Fusiliers by retaining royal-blue facings (i.e. cuffs and collars) on red tunics when full dress and with officers mess dress jackets. However, the distinctive grass-green facings of The Royal Regiment of Wales, which date back to 1717 when Thomas Howard was Colonel of the 24th, is reflected in the design of the Regimental Colour, the drums of the regiment and regimental belts worn by the Colour ensigns, drum major and goat major.

The Goat

Both antecedent regiments of The Royal Welsh marched with a goat at their head. It was apparently a custom of some long standing in the 23rd Foot, when in 1777 Major Robert Donkin, of the regiment, wrote in his *Military Collections and Remarks* that 'The royal regiment of welch Fuzileers has a privilegeous honor of passing in review preceded by a Goat with gilded horns, and adorned with ringlets of flowers;' and that 'the corps values itself much on the ancientness of the custom'.

Queen Victoria gave the first royal goat to the 23rd Foot in 1844. The first goat of the 41st (The Welch) Regiment of Infantry was adopted during the Crimea War (1855), although the reason why a goat was chosen as a mascot is obscure. The first goat from the royal herd was presented to the 41st Foot in 1862. When Welsh battalions were overseas, goats would often come from local sources, such as that presented by the Sultan of Lahej when the 41st Foot was serving in Aden in 1874. The 69th Regiment had no official mascot but, on becoming the 2nd Battalion, The Welch Regiment in 1881, took up the custom. The 24th, South Wales Borderers never adopted the goat as a mascot. On amalgamation in 1969, the last goat of the Welch Regiment was re-named Taffy I of the Royal Regiment of Wales. His official name on the battalion ration register was Gwilym Jenkins.

Whenever possible, the goats are selected from the royal herd which was started at Windsor in the time of Queen Victoria, and is now located at Whipsnade Animal Park. In recent times, when no goat was available from the royal herd, the Queen has been pleased to present a wild goat from the mountains of North Wales, where herds still exist, particularly on the Great Orme at Llandudno. This herd is known to have some Windsor blood in its ancestry.

The goat is in the care of a soldier with the honorary title of Goat Major who wears the traditional white foreign service helmet with green belt over his jacket displaying the regiment's honours. Drawing upon the traditions of the antecedent regiments, in The Royal Welsh, the goat of the 1st Battalion is named 'Billy', 2nd Battalion 'Taffy' and in the 3rd Battalion 'Shenkin'. The term 'mascot' was never used in The Royal Welch Fusiliers. The goats of 2nd and 3rd Battalions are dressed in a green coat with gold piping and regimental crest whilst the goat of the 1st Battalion remains undressed.

The Regimental Motto – Gwell Angau Na Chywilydd

The motto is one of great antiquity and has been used by several distinguished Welsh families, in particular the Mackworth's of Glen Uske, Monmouthshire. The closest translation from the Welsh is 'Better Death than Dishonour' – however 'Rather Death than Dishonour' is more commonly used. It was adopted for the 41st Foot by Lieutenant Colonel Sir Edmund Keynton Williams in 1831, in which year he was successful in linking the 41st to Wales as The 41st or The Welch Regiment of Infantry. The form of the motto originally adopted by the 41st was *Gwell Angau Neu Chwilydd* and appeared as such on 1862 colours. It is interesting to note that the motto of the 2nd Battalion, The

Monmouthshire Regiment, *Gwell Angau na Gwarth* (Better death than Disgrace), taken in use in 1862 by the Monmouthshire Rifle Volunteers, was strikingly similar.

The Wreath of Immortelles

On the return of the 1st Battalion, 24th Regiment from South Africa after the Zulu War, Queen Victoria expressed a wish to see the 'Isandlwana' Colour. On 28th July 1880, at Osborne House on the Isle of Wight, she placed upon the Colour a 'Wreath of Immortelles' (a wreath of dried flowers) to commemorate the devoted gallantry and sacrifice of Lieutenants Melvill (who was the Adjutant) and Coghill and the 'Noble Defence' of Rorke's Drift by B Company of the 2nd Battalion. A letter from the Queen was received by the regiment via Army Headquarters in Horse Guards on 15th December 1880 stating that a facsimile wreath in silver was to be borne around the pike staff of both battalions for ever more. This unique but distinctive honour of carrying a silver wreath attached to the Queen's Colour pike is maintained by regular and territorial battalions of The Royal Welsh.

The Ceremonial Pioneers

Before the days of good roads and bridges and level camp sites, it was necessary to have men who were able to prepare the way for the regiment on the march and to provide services for it at its camps. These were the pioneers, who were all tradesmen and picked soldiers. Their sergeant had to be an outstanding man of great experience. To protect their uniforms they wore leather aprons and gauntlets.

Originating from their role of often leading the battalion on active service, the ceremonial pioneers of the Royal Welch Fusiliers have long held the privilege of marching behind the regimental goat at the head of the regiment on ceremonial parades. They wore white buckskin aprons and gauntlets and carry their traditional axes, shovels, pick axes and a mattock. The apron badge is the enlarged version of The Royal Welsh cap badge, similar to that worn on seal-skin caps. The sergeant traditionally wore a beard.

In 1886, an inspecting general questioned their right to these distinctions of dress, and an appeal was made to the War Office which resulted in a letter, dated 27th January 1887, in which HRH the Duke of Cambridge, Field

Marshal Commanding-in-Chief, was 'pleased to approve of white buckskin aprons and gauntlets being continued to be worn by the pioneers of the 2nd Battalion Royal Welsh Fusiliers, provided no extra expense is incurred against the public'. The tradition of ceremonial pioneers is continued by The Royal Welsh.

Section 13

CUSTOMS, REGIMENTAL DAYS, MUSIC AND PRIVILEGES

Customs

The Loyal Toast

The Loyal Toast was never proposed in the Officers' Mess of the Royal Welch Fusiliers, except on St David's Day. Furthermore, the officers and their guests did not stand when the band played the National Anthem at the conclusion of its programme. This custom has no written origin, but possibly dates from the late eighteenth-century. At the time of the Mutiny at the Nore in 1797 the mutineers called on the warrant officers, NCOs and men of the Royal Welch Fusiliers to join them. Their response was to submit an address to their commanding officer for forwarding to the King, expressing their unswerving loyalty to the Crown. A copy of their address is in the Regimental Museum in Caernarfon, and an endorsement by the commanding officer verifies that it was signed 'by the whole Corps unanimously'. King George IV, at first as Prince of Wales, then as Prince Regent and also as monarch would from time to time dine with the regiment. On one of these occasions, no doubt mindful of the regiment's declaration of loyalty during the mutiny, he is said to have expressed the wish that the Loyal Toast should be dispensed with as 'The loyalty of the Royal Welch is never in doubt'.

Regimental Days

Saint David's Day – Formation Day (1st March)

In a Welsh regiment, this day naturally takes precedence over all others. Military duties permitting, it is marked by ceremonial, sporting and social events with all ranks wearing a leek in their head dress. On that day, the ceremony of eating the leek is observed.

It is safe to assume that St David's Day has been celebrated in the 23rd Regiment since the time of its foundation. One of the traditional toasts is 'Toby Purcell, His Spurs and Saint David.' Toby Purcell was the regiment's second-in-command, who distinguished himself at the Battle of the Boyne in 1690, and his spurs were worn by successive seconds-in-command until they were unfortunately lost in a fire in Montreal in 1842.

The regimental ceremony of eating the leek in the RWF Officers' Mess remained almost unchanged over the years. Major Donkin in his *Military Collections and Remarks* of 1777, recorded that 'Every 1st March being the anniversary of their tutelar Saint, David, the officers give a splendid entertainment to all their welch bretheren; and after the cloth is taken away … the band playing the old tune of, 'The noble race of Shenkin', when a handsome drum-boy, elegantly dressed, mounted on the goat richly caparisoned for the occasion, is led thrice round the table in procession by the drum-major … .' Although no longer ridden, the goat was still led round the table after dinner, followed by a drummer, fifers, (playing *The British Grenadiers*) the drum-major carrying a silver salver on which were leeks, and the mess sergeant with a loving cup charged with champagne. They halted by the latest joined subaltern who, having stood on his chair and placed his right foot on the table, was offered a leek. Whilst he ate the leek, the drummer played a continuous roll until it was completely consumed. The mess sergeant then handed him the loving cup for the toast to 'Saint David'. All those present who had not eaten a leek with the regiment, including guests, were expected to eat one before the party withdrew.

In the Royal Regiment of Wales, before consuming the leek, young subalterns had to lift up their voices in song (or as near as they could get it). They had to sing at least one verse of their chosen opus, with a chorus, in which, they hoped to be assisted by the assembled company. This ordeal over, they devoured the leek as quickly as possible, without taking it from the lips. Next the mess sergeant handed up a goblet filled with beer. The officer raises it in his right hand, while another drum roll is beaten. He then consumed the beer in one draught, toasted '*A Dewi Sant*' (To Saint David) and resumed his seat. Variations of those traditions continue in all officers' messes of The Royal Welsh – Regular, TA and Cadet.

Similar ceremonial is carried out in the Sergeants' Mess, and the Soldiers' dining hall, where the latest joined soldier in each company eats a leek. (The ceremony is intended to be a pleasure and not an ordeal!)

Rorke's Drift Day (22nd January)
To commemorate the 24th's action in the Anglo-Zulu war in 1879 and the immortal defence of Rorke's Drift, at which this regiment was awarded seven Victoria Crosses, soldiers are given a guided tour and an explanation of the Colours and silver held in the officers' mess. The Colours are usually paraded through the barracks during the day and, duties permitting, social events are held in the evening.

Other Anniversaries
Other anniversaries that may be remembered are: Gheluvelt Day (31st October) remembers October 1914 when battalions of the South Wales Borderers and the Welsh Regiment fought side by side, both taking heavy casualties. Other famous joint actions include Alma Day (20th September 1854) when 23rd and 41st fought together in the Crimea, and Waterloo (18th June 1815) where the 23rd and 2/69th were engaged. The battle of Minden (1st August 1759) is remembered in the 23rd as one of the six infantry regiments involved which were later described by historian, Thomas Carlyle as 'those unsurpassable Six, in industrious valour unsurpassable'. The story goes that the six regiments advanced through rose gardens and picked flowers which they stuck in their hats, giving rise to the tradition of the Minden Rose.

Regimental Music

Quick March *Men of Harlech*
The British Grenadiers
Slow March *Men of Glamorgan (Forth to the Battle)*

Other Regimental Music and Songs include:

Ap Shenkin (WELCH and MONS)
God bless the Prince of Wales (RWF and RRW)
Jenny Jones (RWF and WELCH)

Lincolnshire Poacher (RRW)
Scipio (RRW)
St David (RWF)
The Rising of the Lark (WELCH)
The Royal Welch Fusiliers (by John Philip Sousa)
Warwickshire Lads (RRW)

The British Grenadiers is used to march on the Colours and may precede *Men of Harlech* immediately before the eyes right on a parade. *Ap Shenkin* is used to march off the Colours.

Vesper Hymns
Their origins are obscure, but are associated with the 41st, or Welsh Regiment at the time of the first Afghan war of 1842. Known as the Evening or Vesper Hymns they would be played by the band each Sunday or before a ceremonial parade but are now limited to Dinner Nights in the Officers' Mess. They are *Sun of My Soul*, *Spanish Chant* and *Vesper Hymn*.

Privileges

Civic Freedoms (Right of Entry/Liberty)
Local government in Wales was reorganised in 1974 and in 1994 and there is some uncertainty as to whether Freedoms granted by boroughs that no longer exist still apply. By tradition, however, on the formation of The Royal Welsh, the privileges below were deemed to have lapsed and would have to be re-granted by the passing of a resolution within the new authority.

The Royal Welch Fusiliers
Wrexham BC (1946), Caernarvon (1946) (6th Battalion only), Conwy BC (Conway) (1958), Cardiff CC (1973), Arfon BC (Caernarfon) (1975), Delyn BC (Mold) (1976), Wrexham Maelor BC (Wrexham) (1983), Merthyr Tydfil CBC (1994), Swansea CC (1994), Aberystwyth BC (1996) (a Right of Entry), Carmarthen BC (1998), Newport BC (2001), City of Bangor (2005).

The South Wales Borderers and Monmouthshire Regiment
Brecon BC (1947), Newport CBC (1947)

The Welch Regiment
City of Cardiff (1944), Carmarthen BC (1945), Llanelli BC (4th Battalion only) (1950), Swansea CBC (1960)

The Royal Regiment of Wales (24th/41st Foot)
Brecon BC (1969), City of Cardiff (1969), Carmarthen BC (1969), Newport BC (1969), Llanelli BC (1975), Taff-Ely BC (Pontypridd) (1977) (3rd Battalion only), City of Swansea (1981), Dinefwr BC (Llandovery) (1985), Brecknock BC (Brecon) (1989), Warminster (1989) (Liberty), Cynon Valley BC (Aberdare) (1990), Neath Port Talbot CBC (1993), Merthyr Tydfil CBC (1996), Rhondda Cynon Taff CBC (Pontypridd) (2002), Powys CC (Llandrindod Wells) (2003).

The Royal Welsh (date granted)
Cardiff Council (2006) (carried forward), Merthyr Tydfil CBC (2006) (carried forward), Neath Port Talbot CBC (2006), Newport City (2006) (carried forward), Bridgend CBC (2007), Vale of Glamorgan CBC (2007), Wrexham CBC (2007), Rhondda Cynon Taff CBC (2007), Ceredigion CC (2008), Flintshire CC (2008), Powys CC (2008), Swansea City and Borough Council (2008) (carried forward), Gwynedd CC (2008) (carried forward), Carmarthenshire CC (2008), City of Bangor (2010), Brecon TC (2009) (citizenship), Caerphilly CBC (2009), West Cheshire and Chester Council (2010), Conwy CBC (2009), Torfaen CBC (2009), Blaenau Gwent CBC (2010), Denbighshire CC (2010), Caernarfon (Royal Town) 2009, Monmouthshire CC (2011).

BC	Borough Council
CBC	County Borough Council
CC	County Council
TC	Town Council

The Regimental Collect

Eternal God, our heavenly Father, who gave your Son Jesus Christ to die for us and raised him up from the dead; uphold, we pray, the ancient valour of The Royal Welsh, that we may ever follow the path of duty after His example and by his grace be found worthy of your eternal Kingdom; through the same Jesus Christ our Lord. Amen

Dragwyddol Dduw, ein Tad nefol, a roddaist dy Fab lesu Grist i farw drosom a'i godi o'r meirw; erfyniwn arnat gynnal gwroldeb hynafol y Cymry Brenhinol, fel y gallwn bob amser ddilyn llwybr dyletswydd yn ôl ei Esiampl a thrwy Ei ras fod yn deilwng o'th Deyrnas dragwyddol; drwy'r un lesu Grist ein Harglwydd. Amen

Allied Regiments

Canadian Armed Forces
- Le Royal 22e Régiment
- The Ontario Regiment (RCAC)

Australian Military Forces
- The Royal New South Wales Regiment

Pakistan Army
- 4th Battalion, The Baluch Regiment
- 3rd Battalion, The Frontier Force Regiment

Malaysian Armed Forces
- 4th Battalion, The Royal Malay Regiment

South African Defence Forces
- 121 South African Infantry Battalion
- The Pretoria Regiment

BONDS OF FRIENDSHIP

HMS *Trenchant*
SAS *Isandlwana*
The Royal Regiment of Fusiliers
The United States Marine Corps
The Royal Welch Fusiliers in America

WHAT'S IN A NAME

Welch or Welsh

The spelling of Welsh or Welch in the titles of the former regiments does need an explanation. In 1702, when the designation 'Welsh' was granted to the 23rd Foot, the spelling 'Welch' was in common usage, but this was swept away during the latter half of the nineteenth-century by 'Welsh'. In February 1831, a letter was received from Horse Guards directing the 41st Foot to style themselves as 'The 41st, or The Welch Regiment of Infantry'. It would appear that on official publications the spelling varied between 'c' and 's', although both regiments stuck resolutely to the old spelling. Matters came to a head in the Great War, when cap badges were produced for the Royal Welch Fusiliers and the Welch Regiment showing 'Welsh'. Once the war was over, it was generally agreed within the two regiments that the traditional spelling was more correct. Consequently, the two colonels, Lieutenant-General Sir Francis Lloyd and Major-General Sir Thomas Lloyd, made application to the Army Board for the re-instatement of the spelling 'Welch'. Official approval for 'Welch' was received from the War Office on 27th January 1920. This explanation does not however answer the question as to why 'Welsh' is used in the title of the new regiment 'The Royal Welsh'. The assumption is that the Royal Welch Fusiliers were always colloquially referred to as 'The Royal Welch' and some difference was necessary to set the new regiment apart from one of its antecedents. Also, as 'Welsh' is in common usage, any mis-spellings would be minimised.

Nicknames

Throughout history, most British regiments have had a talent for gathering nicknames, the origin of some having now become obscure. The antecedent regiments of The Royal Welsh are no exception. These nicknames provide a colourful, amusing and often less than flattering insight into the regimental character.

The Royal Welch Fusiliers	
	The Nanny Goats
	The Royal Goats
The South Wales Borderers	
	Bengal Tigers
	Howard's Greens
	The Swabs
The Welch Regiment	
	Fogeys or Old Fogeys (41st)
	Invalids or Royal Invalids (41st)
	Travelling Tinkers (41st)
	The Old Agamemnon's (69th)
	The Ups and Downs (69th)
	Lincolnshire Poachers (69th)
	The Grass Pickers (69th)

The 'Old Agamemnons' was a reference to a remark by Admiral Nelson at the battle of St Vincent in 1797. One hundred soldiers of the 69th Foot served with him aboard HMS *Agamemnon* for four years and subsequently transferred with him when he took command of HMS *Captain*.

Senior Major

The term Senior Major is used in both the 1st and 3rd Battalions, The Royal Welsh to describe the appointment of the second-in-command of the battalion. This nomenclature was in common usage in the eighteenth and nineteenth centuries when infantry companies were commanded by captains; there being only two majors in a battalion, the senior one nominally became the battalion's second-in-command.

Fusilier or Private

Private soldiers of the Royal Welch Fusiliers were re-designated as 'Fusiliers' by authority granted in June 1923. The use of this rank continues in the 1st Battalion, The Royal Welsh.

Rorke's Drift Company

The title 'Rorke's Drift' is carried by B Company, 2nd Battalion, The Royal Welsh in recognition of the immortal defence of Rorke's Drift on 22nd/23rd January 1879 by the soldiers of B Company, 2nd Battalion, 24th Regiment under the command of Lieutenant Gonville Bromhead.

Section 14

THE REGIMENTAL ASSOCIATION

For nearly 100 years, comrades associations have, through their network of local branches, provided a focal point for former members of the regiment to meet regularly and co-ordinate support for former soldiers of the regiment who find themselves in difficult circumstances though illness or family hardship. The associations also provide the link with serving soldiers, giving comrades the opportunity to visit the Regular battalions even when serving overseas. An example of these associations is the 24th, South Wales Borderers Comrades Club which was formed on Rorke's Drift Day (23rd/24th January) 1909 at Oudenarde Barracks, Aldershot; the weekend included a reunion dinner hosted by the Sergeants' Mess of the 2nd Battalion. The Comrades Association for the Welch Regiment was formed in January 1911. The Royal Welch Fusiliers Comrades Association first met on 4th October 1912 and the association was formally established by trust deed on 22nd April 1924. The annual membership subscription in those days was 2s 6d (15p). It was not unusual for officers to contribute sizable amounts to what became the beginnings of the regimental benevolent fund. Following the Great War there was considerable pressure on this fund as there was no modern welfare state and work opportunities for former soldiers in Wales were very limited during the depression years of the 1920s and 1930s. The (Royal) British Legion was still in its infancy having only been formed in 1921. It was therefore not unusual to see a payment of 5s 0d (25p) from the fund being made to a former soldier, who found himself on hard times, for the purchase of a pair of working boots. Today, the Regimental Benevolent Fund thrives through the 'day's pay' scheme (DPS).

On 10th June 2010, a unified regimental association known as – The Royal Welsh Regimental Association – was formed and the event was marked by the presentation of two new standards at Chester Racecourse, on the occasion of the review of the regiment by the Colonel-in-Chief. The Association has an active network of local branches. There is some further integration of branches to take place under the guidance of the Association's executive committee.

Section 15

A SELECTION OF PUBLISHED REGIMENTAL HISTORIES

The Royal Welch Fusiliers

Regimental Records of the Royal Welch Fusiliers:

Volume I, 1689–1815, ADL Cary & S McCance, London, 1921 (reprinted 1995

Volume II, 1816–1914, ADL Cary & S McCance, London, 1923, reprinted 1995

Volume III, 1914–1918 (France and Flanders), CH Dudley Ward, London, 1928 (reprinted 1995)

Volume IV, 1914–1918 (Turkey, Bulgaria and Austria), CH Dudley Ward, London, 1929 (reprinted 1995)

Volume VI, 1945–1969, JP Riley, Llandysul, 2001

Volume VII, 1969–2001, JP Riley, Llandysul, 2000

(Volume V, 1919–1945 is in the course of preparation)

Historical Record of the Royal Welch Fusiliers, Major R Broughton-Mainwaring, London, 1889.

The Story of the Royal Welsh Fusiliers, H Avray Tipping, *Country Life*, 1915.

A History of the Royal Welsh Fusiliers, late the Twenty-Third Regiment, Howel Thomas, London, 1916.

A Short History of the Royal Welch Fusiliers, Major EO Skaife, Aldershot, 1924 (new [second] edition); 1927 (third edition); 1940 (reprint with minor changes).

The War Diary (1914–18) of 10th (Service) Battalion Royal Welch Fusiliers, Lieutenant-Colonel FN Burton (Ed), Plymouth, 1926.

The 4th (Denbighshire) Battalion Royal Welsh Fusiliers in the Great War, Captain C Ellis, Wrexham, 1926.

The Historical Records of the Montgomeryshire Yeomanry; with a short account of the service in Palestine and France of the 25th Montgomeryshire and Welsh Horse

Yeomanry Battalion RWF; 1909–1919, Vol II, Colonel RW Williams Wynn & Major WN Stable, Oswestry, 1926.

A Short History of the 6th (Caernarvon and Anglesey) Battalion The Royal Welch Fusiliers, North West Europe, June 1944 to May 1945, Anon, Major HR Roberts MC (Ed), Caernarvon, 1946.

A Brief Record of the Activities of 7th Batt. The Royal Welch Fusiliers, 1908–1946, Major RBS Davies, Llanidloes, 1950.

The Red Dragon, The Story of the Royal Welch Fusiliers, 1919–1945, PK Kemp & John Graves, Aldershot, 1960.

The Royal Welch Fusiliers, 23rd Foot, Major EL Kirby, 1969 (reprinted 1974)

Medal Rolls 23rd Foot – Royal Welch Fusiliers Napoleonic Period, Norman Holme & Major EL Kirby, Caernarfon & London, 1978.

Officers of The Royal Welch Fusiliers (23rd Regiment of Foot) 16 March 1689 to 4 August 1914, by Major EL Kirby, privately published 1997.

That Astonishing Infantry: Three Hundred Years of the History of the Royal Welch Fusiliers, Michael Glover, London 1989, later updated to include history up until 2006 with additional material added by JP Riley, Barnsley, 2008.

White Dragon: The Royal Welch Fusiliers in Bosnia, various authors, JP Riley (Ed), Wrexham, 1995

Fusiliers – Eight Years with the Redcoats in America, Mark Urban, London, 2007

Fix Bayonets! – A Royal Welch Fusiliers at War, 1796–1815: Being the Life and Times of Lt Gen Sir Thomas Pearson CB GCH (1781-1847), Donald E Graves, Stroud, 2007

Dragon Rampant: The Royal Welch Fusiliers at War, 1793–1815, Donald E Graves, Barnsley, 2010

The South Wales Borderers and The Monmouthshire Regiment

The Historical Records of the 24th Regiment, from its Formation, in 1689, G Paton, F Glennie, W Penn-Symons & HB Moffat, London, 1892 (reprinted 2005)

The South Wales Borderers, Jack Adams, London, 1968

The History of The South Wales Borderers: 1914–1918, CT Atkinson, London 1931 (reprinted 1999)

The South Wales Borderers 24th Foot 1689–1937, CT Atkinson, Cambridge 1937

History of The South Wales Borderers and Monmouthshire Regiment 1937–1952:

Part 1. 1st and 2nd Battalions, The South Wales Borderers, GA Brett, Pontypool, 1953

Part II. The 2nd Battalion, The South Wales Borderers: D Day 1944 to 1945, JT Boon, Pontypool, 1955

Part III. The 2nd Battalion, The Monmouthshire Regiment: 1933–1952, GA Brett, Pontypool, 1953

Part IV. The 3rd Battalion, The Monmouthshire Regiment, JJ How, Pontypool, 1954

Part V. The 6th Battalion, The South Wales Borderers: 1940–1945, GA Brett, Pontypool, 1956

A Short History of The South Wales Borderers and Monmouthshire Regiment, Regimental Committee, Brecon, 1959

The Doomed Expedition, The Campaign in Norway 1940, Jack Adams, London, 1989

Shoot to Kill: 1st Battalion South Wales Borderers (Malaya 1950–57), RCH Miers, London 1959

Clash of Empires: 2nd Battalion South Wales Borderers at Tsingtao 1914, John Dixon, Wrexham, 2008.

How Can Man Die Better: The Secrets of Isandlwana Revealed, Lieutenant Colonel Mike Snook, London, 2005

Like Wolves on the Fold: The Defence of Rorke's Drift, Lieutenant Colonel Mike Snook, London, 2006

Surrender Be Damned: A History of the 1/1st Battalion The Monmouthshire Regiment 1914–18, Les Hughes & John Dixon, Cardiff, 1995

A History of the 2nd Battalion Monmouthshire Regiment, GA Brett, Pontypool, 1933

Out Since 14: A History of the 1/2nd Battalion, The Monmouthshire Regiment 1914–19, John Dixon, Abertillery, 2000

On the Western Front: 1/3rd Battalion The Monmouthshire Regiment. Dedicated to the Honoured Memory of Our Comrades who fell in the Great War, 1914–1918, WHB Somerset, HG Tyler & LD Whitehead, Abergavenny, 1926 (reprinted 1999)

With Rifle and Pick: A History of 3rd Battalion Monmouthshire Regiment in the Great War, J & J Dixon, Cardiff, 1991

The Noble 24th: Biographical Records of the 24th Regiment in the Zulu War and the South African Campaigns 1877–1879, Norman Holme, London, 1999

The Welch Regiment

A History of the Services of the 41st (the Welch) Regiment, (now 1st Battalion, the Welch Regiment) From its formation, in 1719, to 1895, DAN Lomax, Devonport, 1899

The History of The Welch Regiment:

Part I. 1719–1914, AC Whitehorn, Cardiff, 1932

Part II. 1914–1918, TO Marden, Cardiff, 1932

A Narrative of the Historical Events connected with The Sixty-Ninth Regiment, WF Butler, London, 1870

A Short History of the Welch Regiment, Regimental Committee, Cardiff, 1938

Cardiff (Pals) Commercial – A History of the 11th (Service) Battalion The Welsh Regiment in the Great War, K Cooper & JE Davies (Eds), Cardiff, 1998

Swansea Pals – A History of the 14th (Service) Battalion The Welsh Regiment in the Great War, Bernard Lewis, Barnsley, 2004

Carmarthen Pals: A History of the 15th (Service) Battalion The Welsh Regiment, 1914–1919, Steven John, Barnsley, 2009

The History of The Welch Regiment 1919–1951, J de Courcy & CEN Lomax, Cardiff, 1952

1/5th Battalion The Welch Regiment – D-Day to VE-Day, Duisburg, 1945 (reprinted 2003)

An Account of the Services of 1st Battalion The Welch Regiment in Korea 1951–1952, Bryn Owen & Norman Salmon (Eds), privately published, 2005

The Royal Regiment of Wales (24th/41st Foot)

A Short History of The Royal Regiment of Wales (24th/41st Foot), Regimental Committee, Cardiff, 1977 (reprinted 1986)

A History of The Royal Regiment of Wales (24th/41st Foot) 1689-1989, JM Brereton, Cardiff, 1989

The Royal Welsh

Welsh Warriors: Operation TELIC 10 (2nd Battalion Battle Group in Iraq), Major Matt Peterson (Ed), Cardiff, 2009

Afghan Dragon: Operation HERRICK 11 (1st Battalion in Afghanistan), Lt Col NJ Lock OBE, *et al*, Wrexham, 2010

Gwell Angau Na Chywilydd (Death Rather Than Dishonour): A Concise History of The Royal Welsh (23rd, 24th, 41st and 69th Foot), Regimental Committee, Wrexham, 2011

General Reading

Mametz – Lloyd George's 'Welsh Army' at the Battle of the Somme, Colin Hughes Guilford, 1990). This book records the events leading to the capture of Mametz Wood by the 38th (Welsh) Division in 1916 in which the following battalions served: 13th, 14th, 15th, 16th and 17th RWF; 10th and 11th SWB; 10th, 13th, 14th, 15th, 16th and 19th Welsh. The author quotes extensively from David Jones, Robert Graves, Siegfried Sassoon and Llewelyn Wyn Griffith, which gives the book a special interest for Royal Welshmen. It also contains extracts from many other personal accounts, collected by the author from all three Welsh regiments.

A History of the 38th (Welsh) Division, Lieutenant Colonel JE Munby CMG DSO (Ed), London, 1920 (reprinted 1991)

History of the 53rd (Welsh) Division TF 1914–1918, Major CH Dudley-Ward DSO MC, Cardiff, 1927

The History of the 53rd (Welsh) Division in the Second World War, Brigadier CN Barclay CBE DSO, London, 1956

Red Crown & Dragon: 53rd Welsh Division North-West Europe, 1944–1945, Patrick Delaforce, Brighton, 1996

The Charge of the Bull: A History of the 11th British Armoured Division in Normandy 1944, Jean Brisset, translated by Thomas Bates, Berkeley, California USA, 1989

The Black Bull: From Normandy to the Baltic with the 11th Armoured Division, Patrick Delaforce, Stroud, Gloucestershire 1993

Taurus Pursuant: A History of 11th Armoured Division, HMSO, London, October 1945

Heart of a Dragon: The VCs of Wales and the Welsh Regiments, 1854–1902, W Alister Williams, Wrexham, 2006

Heart of a Dragon: The VCs of Wales and the Welsh Regiments, 1903–82, W Alister Williams, Wrexham, 2008

A Long Long War: Voices from the British Army in Northern Ireland 1969–1998, Ken Wharton, Solihull, 2008

Footprints on the Sands of Time: The Life of Colonel Harry Morrey Salmon CBE MC

DL DSc (late Welch Regiment), Norman & Hugh Salmon, privately published, 2011

Section 16

SPORTING ACHIEVEMENTS

Since the latter part of the nineteenth-century, the Army authorities have always encouraged their young soldiers to participate in a variety of sporting activities, both individually and as members of teams, it being seen as a good way of offering a physical challenge often to relieve boredom in the quiet overseas postings. The development of these sports, in terms of rules, structure and competitions, mirrored similar developments in the civilian community. Many sports were played and today the diversity is even greater as they can be incorporated into adventurous training activities in different climatic conditions throughout the world. The principal sports within the regiment have been rugby football, association football and boxing. Although in the early years of the twentieth-century, polo was a prominent sport in the South Wales Borderers due to the enthusiasm of one man, Colonel 'Teign' Melvill, son of Lieutenant Teignmouth Melvill VC (who had saved the Queen's Colour after the disaster at Isandlwana), a polo player of international standing who was subsequently awarded an Olympic gold medal at Antwerp in 1920, towards the end of his long sporting career.

Rugby Football

There is no doubt that rugby football has always been regarded as the game of greatest importance in the antecedent regiments of The Royal Welsh, although The Royal Welch Fusiliers came comparatively late to this sport.

The Army Rugby Union (ARU) was formed in 1906 by Lieutenant (later Lieutenant-Colonel) 'Birdie' Partridge of the Welch Regiment; its first Secretary was Lieutenant (later Lieutenant-Colonel) GH Birkett, The South Wales Borderers. It is therefore fitting that the Army Rugby Cup should have been won by the regiment on so many occasions. General Sir Hugh Stockwell (late RWF) was President, ARU for six years in the late 1950s. There have been many rugby successes all over the world; however the army championship

(The Army Cup) is the premier award with the regiment's teams participating in the final on many occasions:

1908 1 WELSH (runners up)
1909 1 WELSH,
2 SWB (runners-up)
1912 2 WELSH (runners up)
1913 2 WELSH
1920 2 WELCH
1921 2 WELCH
1922 2 WELCH
1923 2 WELCH (runners up)
1924 2 WELCH
1925 1 SWB
1926 1 SWB
1927 1 SWB
1928 1 SWB
1935 1 WELCH,
2 SWB (runners up)
1937 1 WELCH
1939 1 WELCH
1954 1 SWB (runners-up)
1955 1 SWB (runners-up)
1956 1 WELCH,
1 RWF (runners-up)
1957 1 WELCH (runners-up)
1969 1 SWB
1970 1 RRW (runners-up)
1971 1 RRW (runners-up)
1972 1 RRW (runners-up)
1974 1 RRW
1976 1 RRW
1977 1 RRW
1979 1 RRW (runners-up)
1980 1 RRW (runners-up)

1985 1 RRW (runners-up)
1986 1 RRW
1990 1 RWF (runners-up)
1991 1 RWF (runners-up)
1992 1 RWF (runners-up)
1997 1 RWF (runners-up)
2000 1 RWF
2001 1 RRW (runners-up)
2003 1 RWF (runners-up)
2006 1 R WELSH (runners-up)
2007 2 R WELSH
2008 2 R WELSH
2010 2 R WELSH
2011 2 R WELSH (runners-up)

The following gained international caps while serving with the regiment:

1903	Lt JEC Partridge, WELCH, South Africa
1920	CSM Charles Jones, WELCH, Wales
1934/35	Lt BTV Cowey, WELCH, Wales
1936	Lt BEW McCall, WELCH, Wales
1939	Lt FJV Ford, WELCH, Wales
1948/49	Pte Windsor Major, WELCH, Wales
1949/50	Pte Windsor Major, WELCH, Wales
1975/76	LCpl Charlie Faulkner, 3 RRW, Wales

2Lt Will Carling gained his first England international cap while serving in the Royal Regiment of Wales on a University Cadetship at Durham University. More than two dozen Welsh Internationals have served with one or other of the former regiments. Many serving members of the regiment have been awarded Army and Combined Services caps, their names being too numerous to mention.

The premier competition in India was the Calcutta Cup presented by the Calcutta Sporting Club which also donated a similar trophy for the England/Scotland international matches. The Calcutta Cup was won in 1917 by a team from the Brecknock Battalion, SWB, that consisted of a number of well-known club players from South Wales serving with the battalion in India.

Association Football

Due to the harder surfaces, association football was a popular sport with battalions stationed in India. The premier all-India competitions were the Durand and Murree Brewery Cups. The Durand was won by 1 SWB in 1900/01 and 1938/39 and the Murree by 1 RWF in 1920, 1 SWB in 1901, 1938 and 1939. Between the two World Wars the Territorial battalions of the Royal Welch Fusiliers competed in at least seven finals of the Territorial Army Association Football competition winning three. In 1938, the 1st and 7th Battalions achieved the unique distinction of being runners-up in their respective finals.

Boxing

Boxing was always popular and among the principal successes was that of 2 RWF in winning the Patiala All-India Boxing Cup in 1911 and 1912. In 1910, 1 SWB won the All-India Cup. In 1925 and 1926, 1 RWF won the All-India Boxing Championship.

Amongst individual successes pride of place must go to Sergeant Johnny Basham, RWF who, in 1914, became the first soldier to win a Lonsdale Belt and, when he won it outright in 1916, became the first man to do so at welterweight. Lance Sergeant Jones, RWF was featherweight champion of the Army 1930–3, Imperial Services champion 1930–2 and Welsh Amateur champion in 1934. More recently, in 1951, Fusilier E Barrow was Welsh featherweight champion, and in 1985–6 Fusilier D Coyle boxed for both the Army and Wales.

During the period 1936–48, the South Wales Borderers produced one of the most outstanding boxers ever to enter an Army ring. Private Edward Richards joined the 2nd Battalion in 1934 and retired 23 years later, after becoming Regimental Sergeant Major – and having earned the sobriquet of 'Killer' Richards. His successes in the ring are too numerous to catalogue here but, at Tunis in 1943, he took part in an American Red Cross tournament to entertain the troops and defeated the American Ezzard Charles, who later became the World Heavyweight Champion.

Other Sports

In 1809, Captain Robert Barclay (Allardice), a well-known eccentric, walked a mile in each hour for a thousand hours, for a wager of 1,000 guineas (£1,050). This feat was emulated in 2003 by Second Lieutenant David Lake, 1 RWF, who, immediately on completing the walk, went on to compete in the London Marathon.

Section 17

THE REGIMENTAL MUSEUMS AND CHAPELS

The history of the regiment is preserved in three fine museums, in Caernarfon, Brecon and Cardiff, and in four regimental chapels in St Giles's Parish Church, Wrexham (The Royal Welch Fusiliers); Brecon Cathedral (The South Wales Borderers); Llandaff Cathedral, Cardiff (The Welch Regiment) and St Cadoc's Church, Trevethin, Pontypool (2nd Battalion, The Monmouthshire Regiment).

St David's Chapel in Llandaff Cathedral was dedicated as the Regimental Chapel of The Royal Welsh on 5th November 2011 whilst retaining its role with The Welch Regiment and The Royal Regiment of Wales.

There are distinctive memorials to the 6th Battalion, The South Wales Borderers and the 1st (Rifle) Battalion, The Monmouthshire Regiment in St Woolos Cathedral, Newport and to the 3rd Battalion, The Monmouthshire Regiment in St Mary's Parish Church, Abergavenny.

The regiment fosters and preserves its strong Welsh heritage and many generations of sons have followed in their fathers' footsteps, making it a family regiment in every sense. Recently, a Society of Friends has been established to support the Museums and they organise a number of interesting events throughout the year. Membership details can be obtained from the museums.

The Royal Welch Fusiliers, Caernarfon

The Royal Welch Fusiliers Regimental Museum is housed in the Queen's Tower of the thirteenth-century castle built by Edward I at Caernarfon. The museum was founded in 1952 at Wrexham and moved to Caernarfon in 1960 on the closure of the Regimental Depot. The displays, which are laid out on five floors, cover the history of the regiment since 1689 and include pictures, prints, weapons, medals, uniforms, insignia and badges, Colours and much more. In 1999, a major redevelopment of the museum was undertaken to incorporate the latest display techniques and systems, project that was supported by regimental fund raising and the Heritage Lottery Fund.

The Royal Welch Fusiliers Regimental Museum, Caernarfon Castle, Caernarfon, Gwynedd, LL55 2AY. Telephone: 01286 673362.
Web: www.rwfmuseum.org.uk

The South Wales Borderers, Brecon

It seems proper that the museum of The South Wales Borderers and The Monmouthshire Regiment should be housed in the oldest building in the Brecon Barracks complex. The museum, created in 1934, was renamed 'The Regimental Museum of The Royal Welsh (Brecon)' in February 2007.

The militia armoury was built in 1805 and contains a wide variety of interesting artefacts, ranging from uniforms and equipment to letters, documents and paintings detailing the history of the regiment from 1689 to its amalgamation with the Welch Regiment in 1969 and onwards to the present as the Royal Regiment of Wales and The Royal Welsh. Donald Morris focused the world's attention on the Zulu War of 1879 through his book *The Washing of the Spears* and Sir Stanley Baker further developed this interest with his film *Zulu*. Nowadays, visitors come from the far ends of the earth to see the great collection of artefacts in the museum's Zulu War room.

The Regimental Museum of The Royal Welsh, The Barracks, Brecon, Powys, LD3 7EB. Telephone: 01874 613310.
Web: www.royalwelsh.org.uk

The Welch Regiment, Cardiff Castle

Between 1975 and 2009, the museum of the Welch Regiment (41st/69th Foot) was housed in the Black and Barbican Towers of Cardiff Castle (artefacts having previously been displayed in Maindy Barracks which provided only limited public access). Of particular interest in the collection are the artefacts relating to the involvement of the 41st in the war of 1812 in North America and in the Crimea and the 2nd Battalion, 69th Foot in the battles of Quatre Bras and Waterloo in 1815. A five-year project to upgrade this museum (and that of 1st The Queen's Dragoon Guards) has now been completed and state of the art displays contain artefacts from both the Brecon and Cardiff museums of the regiment, alongside those from 1st The Queen's Dragoon Guards collection. These are housed in a newly-constructed visitor interpretation centre within the walls of the castle. 'Firing Line: The Cardiff Castle Museum of the Welsh Soldier' was opened to the visitors on 22 February 2010 and officially launched by HRH The Prince of Wales on Armed Forces' Day 26 June 2010. The archives of the Welch Regiment are now held in Brecon.

Firing Line: The Cardiff Castle Museum of the Welsh Soldier, Cardiff Castle, Cardiff, CF10 2RB. Telephone: 029 2022 9367.
Web: www.cardiffcastlemuseum.org.uk

Section 18

THE LITERARY TRADITION

Prior to the Great War and in more recent times some excellent books about its history have been written by its former serving soldiers, namely:

Allan, Major-General, W[illiam], *My Early Soldiering Days – Including the Crimea Campaign*, Edinburgh, 1897 [41st Foot 1850–97]

Allan, Major-General, William, *Crimean Letters from 41st (The Welch) Regiment 1854-56*, W Alister Williams (Ed), Wrexham, 2011 [41st Foot 1850–97]

Anburey, Thomas, Lieutenant, *Travels Through the Interior Parts of North America* (two volumes) 1789. Volume One was edited by Dr Sydney Jackman, FRHistS as *With Burgoyne from Quebec*, Toronto, 1963. [24th Foot 1777–82]

Butler, Lieutenant-General, Sir William F[rancis] KCB, *An Autobiography*, Cape Town, 1911 [69th Foot 1858–98]

Byfield, Shadrack, *Recollections of the War of 1812*, Toronto, 1964 [41st Foot 1804–14]

Cadogan, Colonel, Henry, *The Road to Armageddon – the Life and Letters of Lt-Col Henry Cadogan*, edited by Col Henry Cadogan (grandson), Wrexham, 2009 [RWF 1888–1914]

Lamb, R[oger], late Serjeant in the Royal Welch Fuzileers, *An Original and Authentic Journal of Occurrences during the late American War from its Commencement to the Year 1783*, Dublin, 1809 (reprinted New York 1968)

Latimer, Jon, *1812: War with America*, Cambridge, Massachusets, 2007 [3 RWF 1986–92, 4 RRW 1992–94]

Lysons, General Sir Daniel, *The Crimean War from First to Last*, London, 1895 [1 RWF 1854–56].

Mackenzie, Frederick, *The Diary of Frederick Mackenzie 1775–81*, Cambridge, Massachusets, 1930 [23rd Foot 1756–57]

MacPherson, Andrew John, Lieutenant-Colonel, *Rambling Reminiscences of the*

Punjab Campaign, 1848–9, Chatham, 1889, reprinted 2005, [24th Foot 1842–70].

Richards, Frank, *Old Soldier Sahib*, London, 1936 (frequently reprinted) [2 RWF India 1902–08].

Riley, Jonathon, *The Life and Campaigns of General Hughie Stockwell, from Norway through Burma to Suez*, Barnsley, 2006 [1 RWF]

An amazing outpouring of literature resulted from the Great War, none more so than amongst the Royal Welch Fusiliers. The following list is not exhaustive:

Adams, Bernard, *Nothing of Importance*, London,1917 (reprinted 1988) [1 RWF 1915–16].

Anon [Captain JC Dunn DSO MC* DCM], *The War the Infantry Knew*, London, 1938 (republished 1987 & re-printed 1989) [RMO 2 RWF 1915–18].

Graves, Robert von Ranke, *Goodbye to All That, An Autobiography*, London, 1929 (frequently reprinted) [2 RWF 1915–18].

Graves, Robert von Ranke, edited by Graves, William, *Poems About War*, London, 1988 [2 RWF 1915–18].

Griffith, Llewelyn Wyn, *Up to Mametz*, London, 1931 (reprinted 1981, 1988) [15 RWF / Staff 1915–16].

Jones, David, *In Parenthesis*, London, 1937 (reprinted 1963) [15 RWF 1915–18].

More, John, *With Allenby's Crusaders*, London, (*circa* 1923) [1/6 RWF / HQ 158 Bde 1918–19].

Pinto, Vivian de Sola, *The City that Shone: An Autobiography (1895–1922)*, London, 1969 [6, 19 & 25 RWF 1915–18].

Richards, Frank, *Old Soldiers Never Die*, London, 1933 (frequently reprinted) [2 RWF 1914–18].

Sassoon, Siegfried Loraine, *Memoirs of an Infantry Officer*, London, 1930 (frequently reprinted) [1, 2 & 25 RWF 1915–18].

Sassoon, Siegfried Loraine, *The War Poems of Siegfried Sassoon*, London, 1919.

Silsoe, Brigadier Lord, *Sixty Years a Welsh Territorial*, Llandysul, 1976 [6 RWF / Staff 158 Bde 1914–41].

Vulliamy, CE, *Fusilier Bluff*, London, 1934 [3 & 11 RWF 1918–19].

In the Welsh language, *Private Ellis Humphrey Evans (Hedd Wynn)*, poet and shepherd, from Trawsfynydd in Merionethshire, winner at the National

Eisteddfod in 1917, was tragically killed at Pilckem Ridge in Flanders, while serving with 15th RWF, two weeks before taking the Bardic Chair.

> *Mae gwaedd y bechgyn lond y gwynt,*
> *A'u gwaed yn gymysg efo'r glaw.*
> (They cry is on the wind,
> Their blood is in the rain.)

John Saunders Lewis (1893–1985) is also an outstanding name in twentieth-century Welsh literature and a controversial figure in his nation's politics. He founded *Plaid Cymru* – the Welsh Nationalist party and, in 2005, was voted 10th greatest Welshmen. His letters to Margaret Gilcriest, the Irish woman who later became his wife, covering the period from 1914 to 1924, were edited and published by their daughter in 1993. Saunders Lewis was commissioned into 11th (Service) Battalion, South Wales Borderers during the Great War.

During the Second World War, *Anthony Powell, CH CBE, (1905–2000)*, a sharp observer of the social whirl, painted a matchless panorama of upper-class bohemian life. His 12-volume novel, *A Dance to the Music of Time,* choreographs a cast of more than 300 characters through a rich and melancholy life played out on the margins between high society and bohemia. Powell's father commanded 2nd WELCH during the Great War and he himself served in the Welch Regiment, before transferring to the Intelligence Corps, during the Second World War.

Alun Lewis (1915–44) is one of the most impressive and important writers of the twentieth-century. Perhaps the leading poet of the Second World War, he is still an influential literary figure, particularly in his native Wales. He tragically died at the age of 28 in Burma while serving with 6th Battalion South Wales Borderers.

Arthur (Alun) Gwynne Jones was a regular soldier (who also served with Alun Lewis in Burma). He became a minister in Harold Wilson's cabinet in 1964, taking a life peerage as Lord Chalfont. He published his memoirs, *The Shadow of My Hand,* in 2000.

Appendix A

RECIPIENTS OF THE VICTORIA CROSS

'For Valour'

(in chronological order)

* Posthumous   + Converted Albert Medal

Recipient & unit	*Place*	*Date of Action*
Sgt Luke O'Connor (1/23rd)	Alma, Crimea	20 Sept 1854
	Redan, Sevastopol, Crimea	8 Sept 1855
Capt EWD Bell (1/23rd)	Alma, Crimea	20 Sept 1854
Sergeant A Madden (1/41st)	Little Inkerman, Crimea	26 Oct 1854
Capt H Rowlands (1/41st)	Inkerman, Crimea	5 Nov1854
Asst-Surg WHT Sylvester (1/23rd)	Redan, Sevastopol, Crimea	8 Sept 1855
Cpl R Shields (1/23rd)	Redan, Sevastopol, Crimea	8 Sept 1855
Lieut TB Hackett (1/23rd)	Lucknow, India	18 Nov 1857
Boy G Monger (1/23rd)	Lucknow, India	18 Nov 1857
Pte D Bell (2/24th)	Little Andaman Island	7 May 1867
Pte J Cooper (2/24th)	Little Andaman Island	7 May 1867
Asst-Surg CM Douglas (2/24th)	Little Andaman Island	7 May 1867
Pte W Griffiths (2/24th)	Little Andaman Island	7 May 1867
Pte T Murphy (2/24th)	Little Andaman Island	7 May 1867
Lieutenant The Lord Gifford (2/24th)		
attd Asante Exp. Force	Gold Coast, West Africa	4 Feb 1874
Lieutenant NJA Coghill* (1/24th)	Buffalo River, Natal	22 Jan 1879
Lieutenant T Melvill* (1/24th)	Buffalo River, Natal	22 Jan 1879
Cpl WW Allen (2/24th)	Rorke's Drift, Natal	22–3 Jan 1879
Lieut G Bromhead (2/24th)	Rorke's Drift, Natal	22–3 Jan 1879
Pte F Hitch (2/24th)	Rorke's Drift, Natal	22–3 Jan 1879
Pte AH Hook (2/24th)	Rorke's Drift, Natal	22–3 Jan 1879
Pte R Jones (2/24th)	Rorke's Drift, Natal	22–3 Jan 1879
Pte W Jones (2/24th)	Rorke's Drift, Natal	22–3 Jan 1879

Pte J Williams (2/24th)	Rorke's Drift, Natal	22–3 Jan 1879
Lieut ES Browne (1/24th) attd Mounted Infantry	Khambula, Zululand	29 Mar 1879
L/Cpl WC Fuller (2 WELSH)	Chivy-sur-Aisne, France	14 Sept 1914
Lt-Col CHM Doughty-Wylie* CB CMG (RWF attd Staff MEF)	Gallipoli, Turkey	26 Apr 1915
CSM F Barter MC (1 RWF)	Festubert, France	16 May 1915
Capt A Buchanan MC (4 SWB)	Falauyah Lines, Mesopotamia	5 Apr 1916
Pte JH Fynn (4 SWB)	Sanna-i-Yat, Mesopotamia	9 Apr 1916
2Lieut EK Myles DSO (8 WELSH)	Sanna-i-Yat, Mesopotamia	9 Apr 1916
Cpl JJ Davies (10 RWF)	Delville Wood, France	20 Jul 1916
Pte A Hill (10 RWF)	Delville Wood, France	20 Jul 1916
Pte HW Lewis (11 WELSH)	Macukovo, Salonika	9 Apr 1917
Sgt A White* (2 SWB)	Monchy-le-Preux, France	19 May 1917
Cpl JL Davies* (13 RWF)	Pilckem, Belgium	31 Jul 1917
Sgt I Rees (11 SWB)	Pilckem, Belgium	31 Jul 1917
Cpl J Collins DCM (25 RWF)	Beersheba, Palestine	31 Oct 1917
L/Cpl H Weale (14 RWF)	Bazentin-le-Grand, France	26 Aug 1918
L/Sgt WH Waring* MM (25 RWF)	Ronssoy, France	18 Sept 1918
CSM JH Williams DCM MM (10 SWB)	Villers Outreaux, France	7–8 Oct 1918
Lt–Col DG Johnson DSO MC (SWB attached 2 R SUSSEX)	Sambre Canal, France	4 Nov 1918
Lieut T Watkins (1/5 WELCH)	Barfour, Normandy	16 Aug 1944
Cpl ET Chapman (3 MONS)	Teutoburger Wald, Germany	2 Apr 1945

Associated recipients of the Victoria Cross

Recipient & unit	*Place*	*Date of Action*
Capt CC Lumley (97th, later 2/23rd)	Redan, Sevastopol, Crimea	8 Sept 1855
Lt-Col AS Cobbe (Indian Army, attd 2 KAR, later Colonel SWB)	Erego, Somalilan	6 Oct 1902
Capt JF Russell* MC (RAMC attd 1/6 RWF)	Tel-el-Khuweilfeh, Palestine	6 Nov 1917
Lt-Col D Burges DSO (GLOSTERS, OC 7 SWB)	Grand Couronné, Salonika	18 Sept 1918

RECIPIENTS OF THE GEORGE CROSS

'For Gallantry'

Recipient & unit	*Place*	*Date of Action*
Sgnt A Ford+ (17 RWF)	Gorre, France	30 Mar 1916

Appendix B

COLONELS OF THE REGIMENT

The Royal Welsh Fusiliers (23rd Regiment of Foot)

16 March 1689	Col Henry, 4th Lord Herbert of Chirbury
10 April 1689	Col Charles Herbert
13 July 1691	Col Toby Purcell
20 April 1692	Col Sir John Morgan Bt
28 February 1693	Lieut-Gen Richard Ingoldsby
1 April 1705	Gen Joseph Sabine
23 November 1739	Col Newsham Peers
28 July 1743	Gen John Huske
16 January 1761	Lieut-Gen The Hon George Boscawen
11 May 1775	Gen The Viscount Howe KB
21 April 1786	Gen Richard Grenville
23 April 1823	Gen Sir James Willoughby Gordon Bt PC GCB GCH FRS
31 January 1851	Lieut-Gen Sir George C D'Aguilar KCB
22 May 1855	Lieut-Gen Henry Rainey CB KH
27 December 1860	Gen Sir William J Codrington GCB
16 March 1875	Gen Charles Crutchley
31 March 1898	Gen Sir Edward Earle Gascoigne Bulwer GCB
9 December 1910	Maj-Gen The Hon Sir Savage Lloyd-Mostyn KCB
3 June 1914	Maj-Gen Sir Luke O'Connor VC KCB
2 February 1915	Lieut-Gen Sir Francis Lloyd GCVO KCB DSO
27 February 1926	Lieut-Gen Sir Charles M Dobell KCB CMG DSO
26 October 1938	Maj-Gen J R Minshull-Ford CB DSO MC
3 March 1942	Maj-Gen N Maitland Wilson CB DSO OBE
1 January 1947	Brig Ll AA Alston CBE DSO MC
16 February 1948	Brig Sir Eric O Skaife Kt CB OBE
18 October 1952	Gen Sir Hugh C Stockwell GCB KBE DSO

18 October 1965	Col JET Willes MBE
4 March 1974	Maj-Gen PR Leuchars CBE
4 March 1984	Brig AC Vivian CBE
4 March 1990	Maj-Gen RM Llewellyn CB OBE
4 March 1997	Brig DJ Ross CBE
4 March 2001	Maj-Gen BP Plummer CBE
1 April 2005	Maj-Gen JP Riley DSO

In 2006 became 1st Battalion The Royal Welsh (The Royal Welch Fusiliers)

The South Wales Borderers (24th Regiment of Foot)

8 March 1689	Col Sir Edward Dering Bt
27 September 1689	Col Daniel Dering
1 June 1691	Col Samuel Venner
13 March 1695	Col Louis James le Vasseur, Marquis de Puisar
1 March 1701	Lieut-Gen William Seymour
12 February 1702	Gen John Churchill, Duke of Marlborough KG
25 August 1704	Lieut-Gen William Tatton
9 March 1708	Maj-Gen Gilbert Primrose
10 September 1717	Lieut-Gen Thomas Howard
27 June 1737	Lieut-Gen Thomas Wentworth
21 June 1745	Brig-Gen Daniel Houghton
1 December 1747	Gen William Henry Kerr, Earl of Ancram, Kt
8 February 1752	Lieut-Gen The Hon Edward Cornwallis
15 January 1776	Lieut-Gen William Taylor
13 November 1793	Gen Richard Whyte
19 July 1807	Gen Sir David Baird GCB
7 September 1829	Lieut-Gen Sir James F Lyon KCB GCH
2 November 1842	Gen Robert Ellice
19 June 1856	Lieut-Gen Hon John Finch CB
26 November 1861	Gen Pringle Taylor KH
6 April 1884	Gen Sir Charles H Ellice GCB
13 November 1888	Gen Edmund Wodehouse

29 May 1898	Lieut-Gen RT Glyn CB CMG
22 November 1900	Maj-Gen HJ Degacher CB
26 November 1902	Maj-Gen G Paton CMG
27 February 1922	Gen Sir Alexander S Cobbe VC GCB KCSI DSO
30 June 1931	Maj-Gen Ll IG Morgan-Owen CB CMG CBE DSO
30 June 1944	Maj-Gen DG Johnson VC CB DSO MC
1 January 1950	Gen Sir Alfred R Godwin-Austen KCSI CB OBE MC
18 April 1954	Maj-Gen FRG Matthews CB DSO
1 January 1962	Lieut-Gen Sir David Peel Yates KCB CVO DSO OBE

Merged in 1969 with The Welch Regiment to become 1st Battalion The Royal Regiment of Wales (24th/41st Foot)

41st Regiment of Foot

11 March 1719	Lieut-Gen Edmund Fielding
1 April 1743	Col Tomkyn Wardour
4 March 1752	Lieut-Gen John Parsons
16 May 1764	Maj-Gen Alexander Leslie, The Lord Lindores
6 September 1765	Maj-Gen John Parker
5 August 1771	Lieut-Genl Jorden Wren
14 January 1784	Maj-Gen Archibald McNab
13 January 1790	Gen Sir Thomas Stirling Bt
16 May 1808	Lieut-Gen Hay Macdowell
22 February 1810	Gen Josiah Champagne GCH
14 June 1819	Lieut-Gen The Hon Sir Edward Stopford GCB
26 September 1837	Gen Sir Ralph Daring GCH
5 February 1848	Gen CA Repington CB KH
20 April 1861	Gen Sir Richard England GCB KH
20 January 1883	Gen JE Goodwyn CB (1st Battalion)

Linked in 1881 with 69th Foot to become 1st Battalion The Welsh Regiment

69th Regiment of Foot

23 April 1758	Lieut-Gen Hon Charles Colville
1 September 1775	Lieut-Gen Hon Philip Sherard
19 July 1790	Lieut-Gen Sir Ralph Abercromby KB
26 April 1792	Gen Henry Watson Powell
20 June 1794	Gen Sir Cornelius Cuyler Bt
11 March 1819	Gen Viscount Beresford GCB GCH
15 March 1823	Lieut-Gen Sir John Hamilton Bt KCB KCH
2 January 1836	Gen John Vincent
5 February 1848	Gen Sir Ralph Darling GCH
3 April 1858	Gen Ernest Frederick Gascoigne
19 July 1876	Gen Sir William Montagu Scott McMurdo GCB
23 August 1877	Gen David Elliot Mackirdy

Linked in 1881 with 41st Foot to become 2nd Battalion The Welsh Regiment

The Welsh Regiment

1 July 1881	Gen David Elliot Mackirdy (2nd Battalion)
20 January 1883	Gen Julius Edmund Goodwyn CB (1st Battalion)
16 January 1894	Gen Francis Peyton CB
31 January 1904	Maj-Gen William Allan
13 July 1918	Maj-Gen Sir Alexander Bruce Tulloch KCB CMG
26 May 1920	Maj-Gen Sir Thomas Owen Marden KBE CB CMG
17 January 1941	Maj-Gen Douglas Povah Dickinson CB DSO OBE MC
8 January 1949	Maj-Gen CEN Lomax CB CBE DSO MC
8 January 1958	Lieut-Gen Sir Cyril FC Coleman KCB CMG DSO OBE
20 November 1965	Maj-Gen FH Brooke CB CBE DSO

Merged in 1969 with The South Wales Borderers to become 1st Battalion The Royal Regiment of Wales (24th/41st Foot)

The Royal Regiment of Wales (24th/41st Foot)

11 June 1969	Lieut-Gen Sir David Peel Yates KCB CVO DSO OBE
25 September 1977	Maj-Gen LAD Harrod OBE
1 January 1983	Maj-Gen LAH Napier CB OBE MC DL
1 October 1989	Brig KJ Davey CBE MC DL
1 October 1994	Brig D de G Bromhead CBE LVO
22 October 1999	Maj-Gen CH Elliott CVO CBE
1 November 2004	Brig RHT Aitken CBE

In 2006 became 2nd Battalion The Royal Welsh (The Royal Regiment of Wales)

The Royal Welsh

1 March 2006	Maj-Gen RJM Porter MBE
6 November 2011	Brig PML Napier OBE

Appendix C

LIEUTENANT-COLONELS COMMANDING

1st Battalion The Royal Welsh

Lieutenant Colonel DRH James	1 March 2006–August 2008
Lieutenant Colonel NJ Lock OBE	August 2008–1 March 2011
Lieutenant Colonel SN Webb MC	1 March 2011–

2nd Battalion The Royal Welsh

Lieutenant Colonel JFP Swift OBE	1 March 2006–August 2009
Lieutenant Colonel DM Wheeler	August 2009–November 2011
Lieutenant Colonel CBK Barry	1 November 2011–

3rd Battalion The Royal Welsh (TA)

Lieutenant Colonel MJA Leader	1 March 2006–September 2008
Lieutenant Colonel EM Brain	1 September 2008–1 March 2011
Lieutenant Colonel JW Cleverly	1 March 2011–

Appendix D

CHRONOLOGY OF REGIMENTAL EVENTS SINCE 1689

The antecedent regiments of The Royal Welsh were known by the name of their respective Colonel until 1751. For simplicity in this table, the designation 23rd, 24th, 41st and 69th are used from 1689. Likewise, after 1881, the terms RWF, SWB, WELSH (1881–1920) or WELCH (1920–69), RRW and RWR are used to designate The Royal Welch Fusiliers, The South Wales Borderers, The Welch Regiment, The Royal Regiment of Wales (24th/41st Foot) and The Royal Welsh Regiment (TA) respectively. Also note that the Gregorian calendar was adopted in 1752, when the New Year start date changed from 25 March to 1 January.

1689	Mar 8	Henry, 4th Lord Herbert of Chirbury and Sir Edward Dering, Baronet, of Surrenden in Kent were each commissioned to raise a Regiment of Foot in the service of King William III. These two regiments later became the 23rd and 24th Regiments of Foot
	Mar 16	The first muster of the 23rd at Ludlow, Shropshire
	Mar 28	The first muster of the 24th at Maidstone in Kent
	Apr 10	Charles Herbert, cousin of Lord Herbert appointed Colonel of 23rd
	Jul	24th arrived in Ireland
	Aug 30	23rd arrived in Ireland
	Sep 27	Edward Dering, brother of Sir Edward, appointed Colonel of the 24th
1690	Jul 1	23rd took part in the battle of the Boyne
1691	Jul 1	23rd fought in the battle of Aughrim and death of Colonel Charles Herbert
	Jul 13	Lieutenant-Colonel Toby Purcell promoted to the colonelcy of 23rd
	Dec	24th returned from Ireland and are based in Bridgwater, Glastonbury and Wells in Somerset
	Dec 27	23rd landed in England from Ireland
1692	May	24th based at Guildford

	Aug 1	24th embarked for war with France
1694	Jan	23rd embarked for Holland
	Sep	24th returned to England and to be based in Maidstone, Essex, Suffolk and London
1695	Mar	24th embarked for war with France in Mediterranean
	Jun 21	23rd took part in the siege of Namur. Surrendered 26 August
1696	March	24th returned to London and subsequently based in Gloucestershire, Worcestershire and Herefordshire
1697	Jun 1	24th left for Belgium
	Nov	24th moved to Ireland from Belgium
	Dec 16	23rd landed in England from Holland
1698	Feb 8	23rd embarked for Ireland
1701	Jun 1	24th embarked to Holland from Ireland
	Jul 2	23rd landed in Holland from Ireland
1702	Feb 12	John Churchill, Earl (later Duke) of Marlborough appointed Colonel of the 24th
	Oct 12	23rd participated in capture of Liège
	Dec 15	23rd Regiment formed into a regiment of fusiliers and called 'The Welsh Regiment of Fusiliers'
1703	Aug 25	23rd participated in capture of Huy
1704	May 9	23rd proceeded to Germany
	Jun 21	23rd took part in the battle of Schellenberg
	Aug 2	23rd and 24th fought in the battle of Blenheim
1706	May 12	23rd and 24th fought in the battle of Ramillies
1708	Jun 30	23rd and 24th participated in the battle of Oudenarde
	Aug 13	23rd participated in the siege of Lille. Surrendered 28 November
1709	Jun 26	23rd involved in the siege of Tournai. Surrendered 23 August
	Aug 31	23rd and 24th fought in the battle of Malplaquet
1712		First reference to 'Royal' in the 23rd Regiment's title
1713	Apr 11	Treaty of Utrecht
	Aug 22	23rd landed in Ireland from Holland
	Aug 28	24th landed in Ireland from Holland and was involved in '1715 Rising'
1714	Nov 9	23rd styled 'HRH the Prince of Wales's Own Royal Regiment of Welsh Fuzileers'

1715	Oct 9	23rd arrived in England from Ireland
1717	Sep 10	Thomas Howard, appointed Colonel 24th, an appointment he held for 20 years. The Regiment acquired the nickname 'Howard's Greens' from the colour of their facings
1718	Dec 2	23rd landed in Ireland from England
1719	Mar 1	Edmund Fielding given a commission to raise ten companies using out-Pensioners of the Royal Hospital Chelsea, moved to Portsmouth as garrison troops (later known as 41st Foot). Two companies move to Plymouth 23 June
	May 2	23rd sailed from Ireland for Bristol
	Sep 21	24th involved in the Vigo expedition
	Nov 11	24th returned to Ireland
1730	Oct 30	41st moved to Jersey in the Channel Islands until 3 November 1731 when the regiment returned to Portsmouth
1734	Apr	24th moved to Dunstable, Woburn, Hitchin, Luton and Redborn in Hertfordshire from Ireland
1735	Mar	24th billeted in Abingdon, Cirencester, Wallingford, Witney, Farringdon, Wantage and Highworth
	Apr	24th returned to Ireland
1736	Sep 7	23rd present at the Porteous Riots in Edinburgh
1739	Jun	24th embarked for Jamaica
1741	Apr 9	24th assaulted Fort St Lazare in Spanish West Indies and suffered severe casualties
1742	May	23rd arrived at Ostend from Deptford
	Dec	24th returned to Plymouth, Reading and Wolverhampton
1743	Jun 16	23rd took part in the battle of Dettingen and death of Colonel Peers
	Sep 14	New Colours authorised for 41st as Invalids
1744	Feb	24th moved to St Albans, Barnet and the Tower of London
1745	Apr 30	23rd fought in the battle of Fontenoy
	Jul 9	23rd taken prisoner at Ghent
	Oct	23rd landed in England
1746	Mar 29	24th moved to Fort William, Scotland
1747	Jan 28	23rd landed in the Netherlands
	Jun 21	23rd took part in the battle of Lauffeldt
1748	Oct 7	Treaty of Aix-la-Chapelle

	Dec	23rd landed in Scotland. To England in 1752
1749	Sep	24th moved to Borders; Berwick, Newcastle and Carlisle from Scotland
1750	Aug	24th billeted in Canterbury, Chatham and Dover
1751	May	24th moved to Exeter
	Jul 1	Invalids re-designated as 41st Regiment of Foot (or Invalids)
1752	Jun	24th embarked for Minorca
1754	Apr	23rd embarked for Minorca
1756	Apr 27	23rd and 24th took part in the siege of Fort St Philip, Minorca. Surrendered 29 June
	Aug	1/24th moved to Gibraltar from Minorca
	Aug 24	Strength of 24th augmented by 20 companies and 2/24th formed on 20 September
	Aug 25	2/23rd formed at Leicester
	Nov	1/23rd returned to England
1757	May	1/24th returned to England and to be based in Loughborough, Market Harborough and Melton Mowbray and 2/24th at Leicester
	Apr 8	2/24th involved in expedition to Rochefort under Sir John Mordaunt
1758	Apr 23	2/24th renumbered as 69th Regiment of Foot
	Jun 1	1/23rd, 2/23rd, and 1/24th involved in abortive expedition to St Malo until July
	Jun 25	2/23rd became 68th Regiment of Foot (later the Durham Light Infantry)
	Aug 2	23rd landed in the Netherlands
1759	Mar 29	69th took part in Belle Isle expedition, landed 8 April, returned to England 25 May. First Battle Honour for 69th
	Aug 1	23rd took part in the battle of Minden
	Oct	24th billeted at Dartford, Ipswich, Warley and Chelmsford
1760	Jul 31	23rd and 24th under Lord Granby fought in the battle of Warburg
	Oct 16	23rd involved in the action at Kloster Kampen
1761	Jul 16	24th participated in battle of Vellinghausen
	Dec 24	69th embarked for Carlisle Bay, Barbados, West Indies
1762	Jan 5	69th moved to Martinique from Barbados. Arrived 16 January
	Feb 14	69th embarked for Gibraltar, via Ireland, from Martinique
1763	Mar	23rd returned to England
1764		24th stationed in Gibraltar
1769		24th moved to Ireland from Gibraltar

1773	Mar	41st re-designated as a 'marching' regiment. Presented with New Colours 26 May
	Apr 15	23rd embarked for America. Disembarked New York 11 Jun
1775	Apr 19	23rd involved in the action at Lexington
	Jun 17	23rd fought in the battle of Bunker Hill
	Dec 26	69th embarked for Gosport from Gibraltar. Subsequently billeted at Warley, Essex and Maidstone, Kent
1776	Apr	24th embarked for Canada and Quebec
1777	Jun	British advance from Quebec to New York by General Burgoyne with 24th as leading (or point) battalion
	Oct 7	24th surrendered at Saratoga and many became prisoners of the Convention for three years
1778	Aug	23rd served as marines, until September
1779	May	23rd involved in the capture of Fort Lafayette
1780	Apr 1	23rd involved in the siege of Charleston. Surrendered 11 May
	Aug 16	23rd fought in the action at Camden
1781	Jan 15	69th embarked for Barbados from Gosport
	Mar 15	23rd involved in the action at Guilford Court House
	Jul 16	24th re-formed Tamworth and are billeted at Portsmouth, Winchester, Poole, Dover, Berwick and Edinburgh in next 4 years
	Oct 19	23rd at the capitulation at Yorktown
1782	Jan 14	69th moved to Antigua from Barbados
	Jan 25	69th moved to Basseterre, St Kitts with detachments with the Royal Navy
	Apr 12	69th took part in battle of the Saints off the Island of Dominica. Later awarded a naval Battle Honour
	Aug 6	69th returned to England and were stationed in Dover Castle
	Aug 31	Royal Warrant directs 24th Regiment to style itself the 24th (2nd Warwickshire) Regiment of Foot and locate a detachment for recruiting in Tamworth
1783	Dec 5	23rd sailed for England. Landed 17 January 1784
1784		69th moved to Ireland from Dover Castle
1785		24th moved to Ireland
1787	Sep 29	41st ceased to be 'invalids'
	Dec 25	41st became an infantry regiment of the line

1789	Mar 12	41st presented with new Colours at Hilsea Barracks Portsmouth
	Apr	24th embarked for Canada, based at Montreal, Detroit and Quebec
	May 27	41st moved to Cork, Ireland
1790	Apr 3	23rd embarked for Ireland
1793	Feb 26	69th saw continuous service with the Royal Navy until 1798
	Sep 28	Grenadier & Light companies of 41st moved from Cork to Barbados, West Indies
	Nov 13	23rd flank companies embarked at Cork for Barbados. Arrived 6 January 1794
1794	Feb 3	Grenadier and Light companies of 41st moved to Martinique, St Lucia and Guadeloupe
	Feb 7	69th took part in the Corsica expedition. Until 21 May
	Mar 8	23rd companies embarked at Cork for San Domingo (Haiti/ Dominican Republic). Landed 19 May
	Mar 22	Remaining companies of 41st embarked to Barbados from Cork. Arrived 21 April
	Mar 23	23rd flank companies at surrender of Martinique
	Apr 2	23rd flank companies at capture of Morne Fortuné, St Lucia
	Apr 12	23rd flank companies at capture of Fort la Fleur d'Epée, Guadeloupe
	May 6	41st moved to Martinique from Barbados
	May 19	41st moved to San Domingo
	Jun 1	69th took part with Royal Navy ships in 'The Glorious First of June'
	Jun 3	41st involved in the action and capture of Fort Bizothon, Port-au-Prince, San Domingo
	Jun 4	23rd involved in the capture of Port-au-Prince, San Domingo (Haiti/Dominican Republic)
1796	Jan 1	69th based at San Domingo
	Mar 19	23rd sailed from Port-au-Prince. Landed Spithead 27 April
	May 8	69th embarked for Spithead from San Domingo. Arrived 24 September
	Aug 5	41st embarked at Jamaica for Portsmouth. Arrived 19 October
	Dec 31	41st moved to Cork from Portsmouth
1797	Feb 14	69th took part in battle of Cape St Vincent with Royal Navy. A second naval Battle Honour for 69th
	Jun 6	23rd rejected appeal to join naval mutineers at the Nore
1798	May 19	23rd flank companies landed at Ostend and made prisoner next day

1799	Jun	23rd flank companies rejoined the regiment
	Jun	69th based at Shirley, Southampton until August 1799
	Aug 17	41st embarked for Quebec from Cork. Arrived 24 October
	Aug 27	23rd and 69th involved in expedition to Den Helder. To 29 October. 69th returned to Deal, Kent
	Nov 7	41st moved to Montreal and Upper Canada
	Nov 10	Three 23rd companies lost in shipwreck of the transport *de Valk* off Ameland
1800		69th embarked for Jamaica
	Oct	24th returned from Canada to Plymouth and Exeter
1801	Mar 8	23rd took part in the landing at Aboukir Bay, Egypt
	Jun 4	24th arrived aboard HMS *Monmouth* in Egypt as reinforcements
	Sep 2	Surrender of Alexandria. 23rd and 24th awarded the honour 'Sphinx superscribed Egypt'
	Nov 29	24th returned to Portsmouth
	Dec	23rd arrived at Gibraltar from Egypt, via Malta
1802		1/69th embarked for England from Jamaica and on arrival marched to Nottingham
	Jul 7	2/69th raised
1803	Aug	23rd landed in England from Gibraltar
	Aug 23	41st returned to Quebec
1804	Aug	2/24th re-raised at Warwick for service in Peninsula campaign
	Dec 25	2/23rd raised. Recruited in North Wales
1805	Mar 8	1/69th embarked Portsmouth for India. Arrived 13 July
	May 5	1/24th moved to Cork, Ireland
	Jul 13	1/69th stationed at Fort St George, Madras and subsequently Vellore, Trichonopoly, Madras until December 1808
	Sep 27	1/24th embarked for an expedition to West Indies but are diverted to the Cape
	Oct 29	1/23rd on expedition to North Germany, until February 1806
1806	Jan 8	1/24th landed at the Cape and take part in the battle of Blaauwberg under Sir David Baird. Dutch forces surrender and the Cape is taken by the British. 1/24th stationed at Cape Town
1807	Jul	1/23rd on expedition to Copenhagen. Until October
	Jul 13	General Sir David Baird appointed Colonel of 24th; an appointment he holds for 22 years

	Nov 23	2/23rd embarked at Portsmouth for Ireland
1808	Jan	1/23rd embarked for Nova Scotia. Arrived 16 April
	Sep 9	2/23rd embarked at Cork for Spain
	Dec 6	1/23rd sailed for Barbados from Nova Scotia
1809	Jan 16	2/23rd involved in the battle of Corunna, Spain
	Jan 18	2/23rd embarked for England
	Jan 30	1/23rd landed at Martinique which capitulated 24 February
	Mar	1/23rd returned to Nova Scotia
	Jul	2/23rd in Expedition to Walcheren Island. Until November
	Jul 28	2/24th participated in the battle of Talavera, Spain
1810	Jun 10	1/24th embarked for India and take part in the campaign in Nepal
	Jun 20	69th moved to Rodriguez until 3 July
	Jul 7	69th landed at the Island of Réunion
	Aug 13	69th moved to Mauritius
	Sep 27	2/24th took part in the battle of Busaco, Portugal
	Dec 12	1/23rd disembarked at Lisbon
	Dec 26	69th embarked for Madras from Mauritius
1811	Apr 29	69th moved to Java from Madras
	May 3–5	2/24th took part in the battle of Fuentes d'Onor, Spain
	May 16	1/23rd fought in the battle of Albuhera, Spain
	Sep	41st at Fort George with detachment at Fort Amhurstburg, Quebec and Fort York (Toronto)
	Oct 22	69th moved to Goa, India from Java. Arrived 7 December
1812	Apr 6	1/23rd involved in the capture of Badajoz, Spain
	Jun 24	41st concentrate at Fort George, Niagara
	Jul 3	1/24th Colours lost in Mozambique Channel off Madagascar
	Jul 22	1/23rd and 2/24th fought in the battle of Salamanca, Spain
	Aug 16	1/41st involved in the action at Fort Detroit, Michigan
	Aug 25	2/41st raised at Winchester and move to Chichester and Brighton, Sussex 12 September
	Oct 13	1/41st involved in action at Queenston Heights, Upper Canada
1813		69th moved to Seringapatam, India
	Jan 22	1/41st involved in action at Frenchtown (or Maumee or Miami), Michigan, United States of America
	Jun 21	1/23rd and 2/24th fought in the battle of Vittoria, Spain

	Apr	2/41st embarked for Quebec, Canada. Arrived 15 May
	May 5	1/41st involved in action at Fort Meigs, Ohio
	Jul 11	2/41st based at Fort Niagara, Upper Canada
	Jul 28	1/23rd and 2/24th took part in the battles of the Pyrenees. Until 3 August
	Oct 5	1/41st involved in action at Moravian Town, Upper Canada
	Nov 10	1/23rd and 2/24th took part in the battle of the Nivelle, France
	Dec	1/41st consolidated with 2/41st
	Dec 17	2/69th moved to Williamstadt, Holland from England
1814	Feb 27	1/23rd and 2/24th participated in the battle of Orthes, France
	Apr 10	1/23rd at battle of Toulouse, France
	Mar 8	2/69th involved in the assault on Bergen-op-Zoom
	Jun	1/41st assault Fort Niagara
	Jun 25	1/41st involved in action at Lundy's Lane, Upper Canada
	Jul 16	1/23rd landed in England
	Aug 14	1/41st involved in action at Fort Erie, Upper Canada
	Sep 6	1/69th moved to Bellary with detachment in Hyderabad
	Oct 1	2/41st officially disbanded
	Oct 24	2/23rd disbanded
	Nov	2/24th disbanded
1815	Mar 30	23rd landed at Ostend from Gosport
	Jun 16	2/69th took part in battle of Quatre Bras. King's Colour captured by French 8th Cuirassiers
	Jun 18	23rd and 2/69th took part in the battle of Waterloo
	Jun 24	23rd involved in the capture of Cambrai, France; 41st embarked aboard transport *Lord Cathcart* from Canada, via Spithead (15 July), for Ostend (21 July) and Ghent, Belgium
	Jul 4	23rd arrived in Paris as part of the army of occupation
	Jul 8	2/69th moved to Paris as part of the army of occupation
	Aug 28	41st moved from Belgium to Paris as part of the army of occupation
	Nov 2	41st moved to Ramsgate, Kent from Paris. Arrived 28 December
1816	Mar 28	24th after end of Nepal campaign moved to Amowa
	Feb 16	41st embarked aboard transport *Oceana* for Waterford, Ireland
	Jul 13	24th moved to Dinapore from Amowa
	Jul 25	1/69th moved to Gooty, then Bangalore and Mysore

	Sep 25	2/69th disbandment ordered
	Oct 2	2/69th disbandment completed
1818	Apr 6	69th involved in assault on Wossota in Mahratta war
	May 10	69th involved in assault on Sholapoor. 69th then based at Cannanore on Malabar Coast
	Nov 2	23rd landed at Dover from France
	Nov 19	23rd embarked for Ireland
1819	May 13	69th involved in assault on Copaul Droog during Mahratta war
1820	Nov	41st moved to Scotland from Ireland
1822	Feb 15	41st moved to Gravesend, Kent from Scotland
	Mar 2	41st embarked for Fort St George, Madras from Gravesend. Arrived 6 July. Subsequently involved in the Burmese (Ava) War until 6 March 1824
	Mar 16	Facings of 41st changed from red to white
1823	Feb 5	69th moved to Fort St George, Wallajabad
	Feb 10	24th embarked from India to England
	Jul 2	24th arrived at Portsmouth and are based Gosport and Devonport
	Dec 21	23rd arrived at Gibraltar from Ireland
1824	Apr 14	41st embarked at Madras for Rangoon
1825	Mar 21	Presentation of new Colours to 1/24th at Devonport
	Jul 20	23rd Depot Companies moved to Brecon (moved to Guernsey April-September 1826). Finally moved to Plymouth in June 1830
	Sep 30	24th moved to Ireland and Kilkenny, Limerick, Athlone and Dublin
	Oct 26	69th embarked for Gravesend and stationed at Isle of Wight and Portsmouth. Arrived 26 February 1826
1826	Jun 14	41st returned to Madras
	Aug 14	New Colours presented to 41st at Madras
1827	Jan 20	23rd landed at Lisbon from Gibraltar
	Oct 3	69th moved to Ireland
1828	Mar 22	23rd returned to Gibraltar
1829	Oct 9	24th embarked for Canada and Montreal
1831	Feb 25	Designation of the 41st became 'The 41st or the Welsh Regiment of Infantry'
	June 16	41st authorised to bear the Prince of Wales's plume and motto
	Dec 9	69th embarked from Ireland for the West Indies

1832	Feb 11	41st moved to Moulmein, Burma (with detachments at Mergue and Tavoy)
1834	Nov 10	23rd arrived in England
	Nov 28	The 'Flash' first sanctioned officially for 23rd
1835	Apr 13	41st moved to Arnee, India from Burma. Subsequently to Bellary, Belgaum and Karachi
1836	Sep 16	23rd landed in Dublin from Liverpool
1838	May 25	23rd left Ireland for Canada. Arrived Nova Scotia 12 June
	Aug 4	Presentation of new Colours to 69th at Barbados
1839	Jan 9	69th moved from West Indies to Nova Scotia and New Brunswick
1840	May	24th moved to Kingston, Upper Canada from Montreal
1841	Jun 21	24th embarked for England. Arrived Plymouth 26 July
1842	Feb 20	41st moved to Dadur, India
	Mar 16	41st moved to Quetta
	May 10	41st moved to Kandahar, Afghanistan for first Afghan war
	May 5	Reserve Bn of 23rd formed at Chichester
	May 12	Reserve Bn of 23rd embarked for Canada
	Jul 6	Reserve Bn of 23rd joined 1/23rd in Kingston, Canada
	Aug 29	69th moved from New Brunswick to Ireland
	Sep 5	41st involve in the capture of Ghuzhee
	Oct 8	41st occupied Kabul, Afghanistan
	Oct 11	41st moved to Peshawer from Kabul. Arrived 6 November
	Nov 18	41st moved to Ferozeopore from Peshawer. Arrived 23 December
	Dec 23	41st moved to Hyderabad from Ferozeopore. Arrived 4 February 1843
1843	Mar	41st embarked for Gravesend from India; a party lost off Mauritius arrived in England 16 October 1843
	Jun	41st stationed at Canterbury
	Apr 9	24th moved to Glasgow
	Sep 28	1/23rd sailed for Barbados from Quebec. Arrived 23 October
	Oct 10	24th moved to Ireland, Dublin, Kilkenny and Cork from Glasgow
1844		The first Royal goats presented to each 23rd battalion by Queen Victoria
	Jun	41st stationed in Wales; Headquarters in Brecon, companies at Carmarthen, Newcastle Emlyn, Newtown and Rhayader
1845	Apr 25	69th moved from Ireland to England

	Jun 19	41st moved to Dublin from Cardiff
1846	May 8	24th embarked at Cork for India
	Oct	24th arrived in India, based in Dum-Dum, Calcutta and Ghazipur. 24th was to remain in India until 1861
1847	Mar 5	24th moved to Agra
	Mar 16	1/23rd embarked at Barbados for Nova Scotia. Arrived 2 April
	Nov 22	69th embark aboard transport *Belleisle* at Portsmouth for Malta (arrived 12 December)
1848	Oct 3	24th involved in 2nd Sikh war
	Oct 7	1/23rd landed in England from Nova Scotia
1849	Jan 13	24th attack Sikh guns at battle of Chillianwallah. Queen's Colour lost
	Feb 21	24th took part in the battle of Goojerat
	Apr	24th at the end of the 2nd Sikh campaign moved Wazirabad
1850	May 6	Men and families of Reserve Battalion of 23rd detachment drowned in Lake Erie when *Commerce* sank
1851	Feb 11	41st embarked aboard transport *Hercules* for the Ionian Islands from Cork
	Apr 12	69th moved aboard the transport *Hercules* to Antigua, West Indies and later Barbados from Malta
1852	Dec 2	24th moved to Sialkot, India
1853	Feb 28	41st moved aboard transport *Simoom* to Malta from the Ionian Islands
	Jul 28	Reserve Battalion of 23rd arrived in England and personnel absorbed within 1/23rd
1854	Apr 4	23rd embarked at Southampton for Turkey. Disembarked 25 April at Scutari
	Apr 10	41st embarked aboard transport *Himalaya* at Malta for the Crimea. Disembarked at Scutari on 15 April
	Sep 7	23rd and 41st sailed for the Crimea. Landed 14 September
	Sep 20	23rd and 41st engaged in the battle of the Alma. Two of first Victoria Crosses awarded to Captain Bell and Sergeant O'Connor of 23rd
	Nov 1	24th moved to Peshawar from Sialkot. Arrived 28 Nov
	Nov 5	23rd and 41st fought in the battle of Inkerman Heights. First VC awarded to a Welshman, Captain Hugh Rowlands of the 41st
1855	Sep 8	23rd involved in second assault on the Redan, Sevastopol. Corporal Shields subsequently awarded the Victoria Cross
1856	Jun 17	41st embarked aboard transport *Transit* for England after Crimea

		campaign. Arrived Portsmouth 28 July. Then moved to North Camp, Aldershot
	Jul 21	23rd landed in England from the Crimea
	Jul 29	23rd and 41st with other Crimea battalions reviewed at Aldershot
	Dec 13	24th involved in the suppression of the Mutiny in India until 1858
1857	Apr 3	41st embarked at Portsmouth for Newcastle, Jamaica (with 2 companies in Trinidad and a company in St Lucia)
	May	23rd sailed from Portsmouth. Arrived Calcutta September
	Nov 17	23rd advanced to relief of Lucknow. Lieutenant Hackett and Boy Monger awarded Victoria Crosses. 69th embarked at Plymouth for Alexandria.
	Dec 26	69th arrived at Madras
1858	Jan 9	69th embarked for Rangoon, Burma. Arrived 24 January
	Mar 3	2/23rd re-formed at Newport, Monmouthshire
	Jun 3	2/24th re-formed at Sheffield, Yorkshire
	Jul 2	2/24th moved to Bury in Lancashire
	Sep	2/24th returned to Sheffield
1859	Feb 22	2/23rd arrived at Malta from Portsmouth
	May 3	Presentation of new Colours to 2/24th by Lady Wharncliffe at Sheffield
	Jun	2/24th moved to Aldershot
1860	Feb	2/24th moved to Cork, Ireland from Aldershot where battalion embarked for Mauritius. Arrived 10 March
	Apr	41st Headquarters returned aboard transport *Perseverance* to Aldershot from West Indies. Detachments from Barbados and St Lucia arrived later
1861	Mar 22	1/24th embarked India for England. Arrived 27 July and based in New Barracks, Gosport
		41st moved to Isle of Wight and later Scotland and Ireland
1862	Jan 13	69th moved from Rangoon to Madras
	May 22	1/24th moved to Anglesea Barracks, Portsea from Gosport
	Sep	1/24th moved to North Camp, Aldershot from Portsea
1863	Oct 28	2/23rd arrived at Gibraltar from Malta
1864	Feb 10	69th embarked aboard transport *Trafalgar* for Gosport from Madras
	Apr 28	1/24th moved to Shorncliffe, Dover from Aldershot
1865	Mar 29	1/24th embarked for Ireland and The Curragh Camp, Dublin. Arrived 31 March

	Apr 24	69th moved to North Camp, Aldershot from Gosport. Subsequently moved to Channel Islands
	Jul 24	41st embarked aboard transports *Manchester* and *Albert Victor* for Agra, India
	Aug 5	1/24th moved to Beggers Bush, Dublin from the Curragh
	Oct	2/24th moved to Burma from Mauritius
1866	Feb 22	1/24th return to the Curragh, Dublin
	Jun 21	Presentation of new Colours to 1/24th at the Curragh by Lady Kimberley, wife of the Lord Lieutenant for Ireland
	Jul 13	2/23rd arrived at Montreal from Gibraltar
	Aug 8	1/24th moved to Belfast and Londonderry from the Curragh. Arrived 16 August
	Sep 30	1/24th embarked Ireland for Malta and Fort Verdala
1867	Mar 30	69th moved to The Curragh, Dublin from the Channel Islands
	May 7	Victoria Crosses were awarded to Assistant-Surgeon Douglas and Privates Bell, Cooper, Griffiths and Murphy of 2/24th for saving lives at the Little Andaman Islands
	Aug 19	69th embarked aboard transport *Serapis* for Canada. Quebec, London, Ontario, Hamilton and Montreal
	Oct 29	2/23rd landed in England from Canada. Based in South Wales with 4 companies in Brecon. Until May 1869
1868	Mar 1	1/24th moved to Fort Ricasoli, Malta from Fort Verdala
	Dec	2/24th moved to Secunderabad from Burma
	Dec 4	1/24th (1825-1866) 'Chillianwallah' Colours laid up in St Mary's Church, Warwick (transferred to Brecon Cathedral on 23 August 1936)
1869	Nov 9	1/23rd arrived in England from India
1870	May 31	69th moved to the Citadel, Quebec
	Jun 21	Presentation of new Colours to 69th by HRH The Duke of Connaught at Quebec
	Oct 28	1/23rd moved from Devonport with 5 companies in Brecon. Until 28 September when 1/23rd moved to Pembroke Dock
	Nov 15	69th moved aboard transport *Orontes* to Bermuda from Canada
1872	Feb 29	1/24th embarked at Malta aboard transport *Jumna* for Gibraltar. Arrived 5 March
	Sep 16	2/23rd arrived in Ireland from Portsmouth

	Nov 14	2/24th moved to Warley, Essex from Secunderabad. Arrived January 1873
1873	Apr 5	69th moved Gibraltar from Bermuda
	Jul 1	23rd Regimental Sub-District for 23rd Foot, 24th Regimental Sub-District for 41st and 69th Foot and 25th Regimental Sub-District for 24th Foot established at Wrexham, in Fort Hubberstone, Pembroke (later moved to Cardiff in 1881) and Brecon respectively
	Nov 21	2/23rd embarked at Cork for the Asante Expedition, West Africa
	Dec	2/24th moved to North Camp, Aldershot from Warley
1874	Feb 1	41st moved to Aden from Agra, India
	Mar 20	2/23rd disembarked at Portsmouth from West Africa
	Oct 10	2/23rd embarked at Portsmouth for Gibraltar. Arrived 17 October
	Nov 28	1/24th embarked Gibraltar aboard the transport *Himalaya* for the Cape Town. Arrived 2 Jan and stationed in Wynberg Camp
1875	Mar 5	41st moved aboard transport *Euphrates* to Aldershot from Aden
	May 6	1/24th despatched to Griqualand West to quell disorders in the Diamond Fields
	Jun	2/24th moved to Dover from North Camp, Aldershot
	Oct 7	1/23rd disembarked in Ireland from Portsmouth
	Dec 25	Detachments of 1/24th sent to Port Elizabeth and Eastern Cape
1876	Aug 7	One Company, 1/24th sent to island of St Helena and returned to the Cape 3 August 1877
1877	Jun	2/24th moved to Chatham, Kent from Dover
	Aug 3	1/24th embarked at Cape Town aboard transport *Orontes* for East London and King William's Town in preparation of the Ninth Frontier War
	Aug 17	Companies from 1/23rd and 2/23rd arrived Wrexham to form the 23rd Regimental Depot and Sub-District
1878	Feb 1	2/24th moved to Portsmouth from Chatham and embarked for South Africa aboard the transport *Himalaya*. Arrived East London 9 March
	Mar 14	2/24th deployed on operations in the Eastern Cape until amnesty on 28 June 1878
	Aug 6	2/24th arrived at Pietermaritzburg from King William's Town in preparation for operations in Zululand

	Nov 25	5 Companies of 1/24th disembarked at Port Natal, Durban and reached Pietermaritzburg on 28 Nov in preparation for the Zulu campaign 1879
	Jan 11	HQ and 4 Companies 1/24th and 2/24th crossed the Buffalo River into Zululand
	Jan 22	4 Companies 1/24th and 1 Company 2/24th overwhelmed by superior Zulu forces at Isandlwana: 21 officers and 575 men killed; only 10 soldiers from 1/24th escaped. Lts Mevill and Coghill saved Queen's Colour 1/24th. Colours 2/24th lost. Rorke's Drift post defended by B Company 2/24th stood firm against repeated Zulu over 12 hours. Later, seven VCs awarded to men of 2/24th
	Feb 4	Bodies of Lts Melvill and Coghill found and buried. Queen's Colour 1/24th recovered from Buffalo River
	Mar 1	Draft of 500 men embarked at Woolwich aboard transport *Clyde* to reinforce 1/24th and 2/24th. Arrived Port Natal, Durban 11 April
	May 9	1/23rd returned to England from Ireland
	May 14	Re-constituted 1/24th left Dundee, Natal for second invasion of Zululand. 2/24th employed on constructing temporary forts along the route
	Jun 3	2/24th provided Guard of Honour and escort for the mortal remains of the Prince Imperial of France
	Jul 4	The 5 companies of the 1/24th guarded the entrenched camp on the White Umvolozi river during the final battle of Ulundi
	Jul	41st moved to Gibraltar from Aldershot
	Aug 27	1/24th embarked at Durban aboard the transport *Egypt* for England. Arrived at Portsmouth and inspected by the Commander-in-Chief, HRH Duke of Cambridge. 1/24th proceeded to New Barracks, Gosport
	Oct 21	2/24th embarked at Port Natal, Durban aboard the transport *Orontes* for Casemate Barracks, Gibraltar. Arrived 12 February
	Nov 21	69th moved to Sheffield, Yorkshire from Gibraltar
1880	Feb 21	2/23rd arrived at Plymouth from Gibraltar
	Mar 1	1/23rd, 2/23rd and Regimental Depot officers dined together at Woolwich
	Jul 28	The Queen's Colour 1/24th, recovered from the Buffalo river, was taken and presented to HM Queen Victoria at Osborne House, when

		she attached the Wreath of Immortelles (dried flowers) to the pike
	Apr 29	24th officially adopts *The Men of Harlech* as the regiment's quick march
	Aug 3	41st embarked at Portsmouth abroad transport *Orontes* for Gibraltar. Arrived 10 August.
	Aug 6	Presentation of new Colours to 2/24th by Lord Napier at Gibraltar to replace those lost in the Zulu campaign
	Aug 10	2/24th embarked at Gibraltar aboard the transport *Orontes* for Secunderabad, India. Arrived 16 September
	Aug 16	1/23rd embarked for India. Arrived Bombay 12 September
	Nov	1/24th moved to Colchester from Gosport
	Dec 15	Authority received for a silver wreath to be borne on the Queen's Colour pike of both Battalions of the 24th
1881	Mar 13	1/41st embarked aboard RMS *Grantully Castle* at Gibraltar for Durban, Natal. Arrived 2 April
	Mar 15	Remains of 1859 2/24th (Zulu War) Colours deposited at Windsor Castle
	Jul 1	1/24th and 2/24th re-designated as 1st and 2nd Battalions The South Wales Borderers, and 1/41st and 1/69th as 1st and 2nd Battalions The Welsh Regiment. Regimental Sub-Districts in Brecon and Cardiff renumbered as 24th and 41st Sub-Districts
1882	Aug	1 SWB moved to Manchester from Colchester
	Dec 21	1 WELSH moved to Pietermaritzburg and Zululand with companies in Mauritius
1883	Feb 22	2 WELSH moved to northern Ireland from Sheffield
	May 1	Presentation of new Colours to 4 SWB (Militia) by the Earl of Powis at Welshpool
	Sep 26	1 SWB moved to Kilkenny, Ireland from Manchester
	Nov 20	2 RWF moved to Ireland from Pembroke Dock
	Dec 31	2 SWB moved to Bangalore from Secunderabad
1884	Feb	2 SWB moved to Madras from Bangalore
	Apr 19	2 WELSH moved to Mullingar, Ireland from Londonderry
	June 3	Presentation of new Colours to 3 SWB (Militia) by Lady Ormathwaite at Slwch Camp, Brecon
1885	May 21	Presentation of new Colours to 4 RWF (Militia) by Mrs H Platt at Cae Toplis, Caernarvon

	Sep	1 SWB moved to The Curragh, Dublin
	Nov 2	1 RWF left Calcutta for Burma
	Nov 28	1 RWF entered Mandalay
1886	May	2 SWB moved on operations in Burma from Madras
	May 9	1 WELSH embarked at Durban aboard transport *Jumna* for Egypt and Suakin
	Oct	1 SWB moved to Birr from The Curragh, Dublin
1887	Mar 24	1 RWF returned to India
	Sep	1 SWB returned to Dublin
1888	Nov 10	2 SWB returned from Burma via Rangoon and Calcutta aboard Indian merchantman *Clive* to Bureilly and Ranikhet
1889	Aug 22	1 WELSH embarked at Alexandria aboard transport *Himalaya* for Malta
	Dec	1 SWB moved to Aldershot from Dublin
1890	Dec	2 SWB move to Allahabad from Ranikhet
1891	Feb 6	2 WELSH embarked for Devonport from Queenstown (Cobh)
	Mar	1 RWF took part in the Black Mountain Expedition (Hazara)
1892	Sep 2	2 RWF arrived at Holyhead from Ireland and marched through North Wales
	Sep 13	2 WELSH moved to Malta from Portsmouth aboard transport *Serapis*. The first meeting of 1 WELSH and 2 WELSH. Later same year 2 WELSH moved to Secunderabad, India (arrived 16 October)
	Oct	2 SWB moved to Aden from Allahabad, India
	Dec	1 SWB embarked England for Cairo. Arrived 9 February
1893	Mar 14	First edition of the Regimental Journal *The Men of Harlech* published by 2 WELSH in Trimulgherry, Deccan, India
	Oct 27	2 SWB embarked at Aden aboard the transport *Malabar* for Portsmouth. Arrived 18 November
	Nov 14	1 WELSH moved to Pembroke Dock from Malta aboard transport *Himalaya*. Subsequently to Cardiff, Plymouth and Aldershot. Arrived 19 November
1895	Apr 19	1 SWB moved to Gibraltar from Cairo. Arrived 19 April
	Aug 31	2 SWB moved to Aldershot from Gosport
1896	Jul 16	2 RWF arrived at Malta from England
	Oct 28	1 RWF arrived at Aden from India
1897	Apr 9	2 RWF landed at Candia, Crete

	Jul 9	2 SWB moved to Lanion Barracks, Pembroke Dock from Aldershot
	Nov	1 SWB moved to Meerut, India from Gibraltar. Arrived 10 December
	Dec 9	1 RWF arrived in England from Aden
1898	Jan 23	Unveiling of the Zulu War memorial tablet to the 24th in Brecon Priory Church
	Mar	1 SWB moved to Chakrata from Meerut
	Aug 6	2 RWF arrived in Cairo from Crete
	Sep	2 RWF returned to Crete until December
1899	Jan 13	2 RWF arrived in Hong Kong from Crete
	Sep 4	2 SWB moved to Dublin from Pembroke Dock
	Oct 23	1 RWF embarked for South Africa. Arrived Durban 17 November
	Nov 4	1 WELSH embarked for South Africa. Arrived Port Elizabeth, Eastern Cape 26 November, joined 18th Brigade, part of 4th Division
	Nov 13	Presentation of new Colours by HE Lord Curzon to 2 WELSH at Ahmednaga
	Nov	1 SWB moved to Dehra Dun and Pru, India
	Dec 3	3 WELSH mobilised at Cardiff
	Dec 15	1 RWF involved in battle of Colenso
	Dec 22	2 SWB moved to Badajos Barracks, Aldershot from Dublin prior to embarking to South Africa. Arrived Cape Town 3 February. Part of 15 Brigade, 7th Division
1900	Jan 12	2 SWB embarked at Southampton aboard SS *Bavarian* for Cape Town. 3 WELSH embarked for South Africa, arrived 1 March
	Jan 23	3 SWB mobilised at Brecon and moved to Dublin
	Feb 14	3 SWB embarked at Queenstown (Cobh), Ireland for South Africa. Arrived Cape Town 8 March
	Feb 15	1 WELSH at the Relief of Kimberley
	Feb 17–27	1 WELSH involved at Paardeberg
	Feb 28	1 RWF at the Relief of Ladysmith
	Mar 13	1 WELSH entered Bloemfontein
	Mar	1 SWB moved to Meerut
	May 31	1 WELSH entered Johannesburg
	Jun 2	All ranks of the regular RWF battalions authorized to wear the Flash on full dress
	Jun 5	1 WELSH entered Pretoria

	Jun 22	2 RWF at relief of Tientsin, China
	Aug 14	2 RWF at relief of Peking
	Nov	1 SWB moved to Peshawar
	Nov 3	2 RWF arrived back in Hong Kong
1901	Mar 14	2 RWF (4 Companies) embarked for Tientsin, China
	Dec 21	HRH Prince of Wales (later King George V) to be Colonel-in-Chief, RWF
1902	Feb 8	3 WELSH embarked for England. Disembodied at Cardiff 8 March
	Mar 1	3 SWB embarked Cape Town for Southampton
	Oct	1 SWB moved to Mian Mir and Umballa
	Nov	1 SWB moved to Delhi Durbar events
	Nov 10	2 RWF embarked at Hong Kong for India. Arrived 24 November. To Meerut
1903	Jan 1	1 SWB and 1 WELSH took part in the Delhi Durbar
	Jan	1 SWB moved to Mian Mir and Dalhousie
	Feb 4	1 RWF arrived in England from South Africa
1904	May 20	2 SWB embarked at Cape Town for Southampton. Arrived Bulford, Wiltshire 9 June
	Jul 14	1 WELSH embarked aboard the transport *Dilwara* for Gravesend from Durban (arrived 8 August)
	Nov 26	2 RWF arrived at Agra
	Dec 3	2 SWB moved to newly built Aliwal Barracks, Tidworth from Bulford
1905	Mar	1 SWB moved to Karachi and Hyderabad
1906	Jul 23	1 WELSH moved to Bordon from Gravesend
	Oct 4	2 WELSH embarked for Bloemfontein, South Africa from Karachi
	Oct 12	2 SWB moved to Oudenarde Barracks, Aldershot
1907	Oct 2	1 RWF arrived in Ireland
	Dec 15	2 RWF sailed from Calcutta for Rangoon, Burma. To Shwebo
1908	Apr 1	Territorial Force (TF) established. From existing volunteer Bns: 4 RWF, 5 RWF, 6 RWF, 7 RWF, Brecknockshire Bn SWB, 1st, 2nd, 3rd Monmouths, 4 WELSH, 5 WELSH, 6 WELSH and 7 WELSH formed
	Aug 4	4 SWB (Militia) Colours (1881–1908) laid up in St Mary's Church, Welshpool
	Oct 7	1 WELSH moved to Pembroke Dock from Bordon
1909	Jan 23	1st gathering of SWB Comrades Club at Oudenarde Barracks,

		Aldershot
	Mar	1 SWB moved to Roberts Barracks, Quetta
	Jun 19	Presentation of first Colours to Territorial Force battalions 4 RWF, 5 RWF, 6 RWF, 7 RWF, Brecknockshire Bn SWB, 5 WELSH, 6 WELSH, 2nd Monmouths and 3rd Monmouths by HM King Edward VII in Windsor Great Park
	Sep 13	2 SWB moved to Chatham from Aldershot
	Dec 10	1 WELSH embarked for Alexandria, Egypt with a detachment in Cyprus from Southampton
1910	Feb 22	2 WELSH embarked aboard transport *Braemar Castle* at Durban, South Africa for Pembroke Dock
	Jul 30	Presentation of first Colours to 4 WELSH at Aberystwyth
	Dec 2	1 SWB embarked for England and Lower Barracks, Chatham. Arrived 23 December
	Dec 13	Presentation of new Colours to 1 WELSH at Mustapha Pasha Barracks, Alexandria, Egypt by Lord Kitchener
	Dec 21	2 SWB embarked aboard the transport *Soudan* for South Africa. Arrived Artillery Barracks, Pretoria 15 January
1911	Jan 9	2 RWF arrived back in India from Burma
1912	Oct	2 SWB departed Durban aboard the transport *Soudan* for China. Arrived Tientsin 3 November
	Sep 25	2 WELSH moved to Bordon from Pembroke Dock
	Nov 21	1 RWF landed in England from Ireland
1913	Feb 6	1 WELSH moved to Khartoum from Cairo
	Sep 28	1 SWB moved to Martinique Barracks Bordon from Chatham
1914	Jan 10	1 RWF embarked at Southampton for Malta. Arrived 17 January
	Feb 14	1 WELSH moved to Karachi from Khartoum
	Feb 17	2 RWF sailed from Karachi for England
	Mar 2	1 RWF and 2 RWF met at Malta
	Mar 4	Memorial to the 24th unveiled by General Sir Reginald Hart VC on the battlefield of Isandlwana
	Mar 10	2 RWF landed at Southampton from India. To Portland
	Mar 28	1 WELSH moved to Chakrata from Meerut
	Aug 4	Start of the Great War
	Sep 12	1 RWF arrived at Southampton from Malta

Nov 19	2 SWB departed Tsingtao after German surrender
Nov 20	1 WELSH embarked at Karachi for Plymouth

During the Great War, the Royal Welsh Fusiliers is credited with 40 battalions, 22 of which served overseas in the following operational theatres (dates of arrival in theatre shown in brackets):

1st	France and Flanders (Oct 1914), and Italy (1917)
2nd	France and Flanders (Aug 1914)
4th	France and Flanders (Nov 1914) initially as infantry later as pioneers to 47th Division
5th	Gallipoli (1915), Egypt (1916) and Palestine (1917), part of 53rd (Welsh) Division
6th	Gallipoli (1915), Egypt (1916) and Palestine (1917), part of 53rd (Welsh) Division
7th	Gallipoli (1915), Egypt (1916) and Palestine (1917), part of 53rd (Welsh) Division
8th	Gallipoli (1915), Egypt (1916) and Mesopotamia (1917)
9th	France and Flanders (1915)
10th	France and Flanders (1915)
11th	France (Sep 1915) and Salonika (Nov 1915)
13th	France and Flanders (1915), part of 38th (Welsh) Division
14th	France and Flanders (1915), part of 38th (Welsh) Division
15th (London Welsh)	France and Flanders (1915), part of 38th (Welsh) Division
16th	France and Flanders (1915), part of 38th (Welsh) Division
17th	France and Flanders (1915), part of 38th (Welsh) Division
19th (Bantam)	France and Flanders (1916)
24th (Denbs Yeo)	Egypt, Palestine (1917) and France (1918)
25th (Mont & Welsh Horse Yeo)	Egypt, Palestine (1917) and France (1918)
1st Garrison	Gibraltar (1915)
2nd Garrison	Egypt (1916)
4th Garrison (later 26th)	France and Flanders (1916)
6th Garrison	Egypt (1917) and Salonika (1918)

During the Great War, the South Wales Borderers and Monmouthshire Regiment are credited with 31 battalions, 17 of which served overseas in the following operational theatres (dates of arrival in theatre shown in brackets):

1st	France and Flanders (Aug 1914)
2nd	Tsingtao (Sep 1914), Gallipoli (Apr 1915), France and Flanders (Mar 1916)
4th	Gallipoli (Jul 1915), Mesopotamia (1916)
5th	France and Flanders (Jul 1915) as pioneers to 19th Division
6th	France and Flanders (Sep 1915) as pioneers to 30th Division
7th	France and Flanders (Sep 1915), Salonika (Nov 1915)
8th	France and Flanders (Sep 1915), Salonika (Nov 1915)
10th	France and Flanders (Dec 1915), part of 38th (Welsh) Division
11th	France and Flanders (Dec 1915), part of 38th (Welsh) Division
12th (Bantam)	France and Flanders (Jun 1916)
51st	Army of Occupation on the Rhine, Germany (Mar–Aug 1919), Southern Ireland (1919)
52nd	Army of Occupation on the Rhine, Germany (Mar–Aug 1919), Southern Ireland (1919)
53rd	Army of Occupation on the Rhine, Germany (Mar–Aug 1919), Southern Ireland (1919)
1/1 Brecknocks	Aden (Dec 1914), India (Aug 1915)
1st Mons	France and Flanders (Feb 1915), initially as infantry later as pioneers to 46th Division
2nd Mons	France and Flanders (Nov 1914), initially as infantry later as pioneers to 29th Division
3rd Mons	France and Flanders (Feb 1915), initially as infantry later as pioneers. Disbanded in August 1916

During the Great War, the Welsh Regiment is credited with 34 battalions, 21 of which served overseas in the following operational theatres (dates of arrival in theatre shown in brackets):

1st	France and Flanders (Jan 1915), Salonika (Nov 1915)
2nd	France and Flanders (Aug 1914)
4th	Gallipoli (1915), Palestine (1916) as part of 53rd (Welsh) Division
5th	Gallipoli (1915), Palestine (1916) as part of 53rd (Welsh) Division
6th	France and Flanders (Oct 1914)
8th	Gallipoli (1915), Mesopotamia (1916)
9th	France and Flanders (1915)
10th	France and Flanders (1915)
11th	France and Flanders (Sep 1915), Salonika (Nov 1915)
13th	France and Flanders (1915) as part of 38th (Welsh) Division
14th	France and Flanders (1915) as part of 38th (Welsh) Division
15th	France and Flanders (1915) as part of 38th (Welsh) Division
16th	France and Flanders (1915) as part of 38th (Welsh) Division
17th	France and Flanders (1916)
18th (Bantam)	France and Flanders (1916)
19th	France and Flanders (1915) as pioneers to 43rd Division
23rd	Salonika (1916) as pioneers to 28th Division
24th (Pembs & Glam Yeo)	Palestine (1915), France and Flanders (1918)
51st	Army of Occupation on the Rhine (1919)
52nd	Army of Occupation on the Rhine (1919)
53rd	Army of Occupation on the Rhine (1919)

1919	Mar 25	1 WELSH embarked at Gallipoli for UK
	Mar 29	2 WELSH departed Dunkirk for Southampton
	Apr 4	2 SWB re-constituted from cadre strength at Brecon
	Apr 17	1 WELSH and 2 WELSH re-constituted from cadre strength at Cardiff and Llanion Barracks, Pembroke Dock
	Apr 24	1 RWF re-formed at Park Hall Camp, Oswestry

	Jun 13	1 SWB re-constituted from cadre strength by personnel from 3 SWB at Canterbury
	Jun 20	1 SWB moved to Brecon
	Jul 1	2 WELSH moved to Fort Darland, Chatham and absorbs drafts from 3 WELSH
	Aug 6	2 RWF arrived in Limerick, Ireland from Wrexham and absorbed 3 RWF
	Aug 19	1 WELSH embarked at Liverpool aboard transport *Ixion* for India
	Aug 31	1 SWB moved to Chatham from Brecon
	Sep 15	2 WELSH moved to Llanion Barracks, Pembroke Dock. Deployed to Swansea during Railway Strike
	Sep	1 WELSH stationed at Gough Barracks, Secunderabad
	Oct 15	1 SWB moved to Blackdown Camp, Hampshire
	Oct 21	2 SWB sailed from Liverpool for India aboard transport *Medic*. Arrived Jhansi 23 November
	Oct 25	1 RWF sailed from Liverpool for India on transport *Northumberland*. Arrived Lucknow 17 November
	Nov 1	1 WELSH moved to Gough Barracks, Ferozepore
1920	Feb	Spelling 'Welch' in title of regiment approved for RWF and WELCH (Army Order 56)
	Jun 20	1 SWB embarked for Ireland and Dollymount Camp, Dublin
	Jun 21	2 WELCH moved to Kilmainham Jail then Richmond Barracks, Dublin
	Sep 21	1 SWB deployed during the troubles in Ireland in County Meath
1921	Dec 12	1 RWF arrived at Ladha, Waziristan from Lucknow
1922	Feb 10	1 SWB moved to Alma Barracks, Blackdown
	Mar 21	2 RWF arrived The Curragh from Limerick. Then Dublin 15 May
	May 25	Regimental Chapel dedicated in Brecon Cathedral. The Great War Service battalions Union Colours laid up. The Great War Roll of Honour unveiled
	Aug 11	HRH The Prince of Wales appointed first Colonel-in-Chief SWB
	Nov 1	1 WELCH moved to Roberts Barracks, Peshawar
	Nov 22	2 SWB moved to Barrackpore and Dum Dum from Jhansi
	Dec 14	2 WELCH move to Sobraon Barracks, Colchester from Dublin
	Dec 15	2 RWF arrived at Pembroke Dock from Ireland
1923	Mar 5	1 WELCH marched from Peshawar to Razmak. Arrived 13 March

	Apr 23–5	1 RWF arrived at Multan, Lahore District from Ladha
	Jun	The use of the rank Fusilier for private soldiers in the RWF approved (Army Order 222)
	Jul 25	Remains of 1859 Zulu War Colours 2/24th returned to the Regiment. Placed in the Regimental Chapel, Brecon Cathedral on 20 April 1924
	Sep 23	1 SWB moved to South Raglan Barracks, Devonport
1924	Jan	The wearing of the Flash on service dress by other ranks in the RWF approved (Army Council Instruction 62)
	Oct 21	2 WELCH moved to Candahar Barracks, Tidworth
	Nov 11	General Sir Thomas Marden unveiled the memorial to the fallen of 1 WELCH and 2 WELCH during the Great War at entrance of Maindy Barracks along with 'Stick it the Welch' within the barracks
	Nov 19	1 WELCH moved to Hyde Barracks, Bareilly
1925	Apr 1	2 SWB moved to Lebong from Barrackpore
	Aug	2 RWF on Public Duties, London
	Nov 22	Memorial tablet unveiled in St Luke's Church, Dinapore in memory of the 202 officers, NCOs, men and women and children of 1/24th who died between 1816 and 1818
	Dec 4	2 SWB moved to Agra from Lebong
	Dec 22	1 RWF arrived at Nasirabad, Rajputana from Multan
1926	May 1	1 SWB embarked at Devonport aboard transport *Neuralia* for Liverpool to assist civil powers during national strike. Arrived 3 May and Battalion encamped at Altcar Camp; later moved to Bury, Lancashire. Battalion returned to Devonport 7 December
	Nov 10	2 RWF arrived at Bingen, BAOR from Pembroke Dock
1927	Feb 8	1 SWB moved to Whittington Barracks, Lichfield from Devonport
	Mar 5	1 WELCH embarked at Karachi aboard transport *City of Marseilles* for Aden. Arrived 10 March
	Apr 11	2 WELCH moved to Hong Kong aboard transport *Derbyshire* from Tidworth. Arrived 15 May
	Apr 30	RWF Alliance with 1st Battalion Australian Military Forces authorized
	Jun 30	RWF Alliance with 12th Infantry (Pretoria Regiment) authorized
	Jul 31	RWF Alliance with the Royal 22ème Régiment of Canada authorized
	Sep 3	2 WELCH arrived aboard transport *Herminius* at Shanghai, China
	Oct 12	2 RWF moved from Bingen to Biebrich, Wiesbaden

	Nov 1	2 SWB moved to Bombay by train and embarked on 3 November
	Nov 9	1 WELCH embarked at Aden aboard transport *Neuralia* for New Barracks, Gosport. Arrived 25 November
	Nov 10	2 SWB disembarked at Aden
1928	Jan 23	1 RWF arrived at Quetta from Nasirabad
	Sep 18	1 SWB embarked at Southampton aboard transport *Dorsetshire* for Cairo. Arrived Port Said 30 September
	Sep 20	HRH The Prince of Wales, Colonel-in-Chief SWB, visits 2 SWB in Aden
	Nov 11	2 WELCH moved to Tanglin Barracks, Singapore aboard transport *Somersetshire* from Shanghai
1929	Jan 21	2 SWB embarked for England aboard transport *Nevasa* at Aden. Arrived Victoria Barracks, Portsmouth on 16 February
	May 5	Regimental memorial unveiled to 1 SWB at Gheluvelt, Belgium
	Aug 25	1 SWB deployed to Palestine during disturbances from Cairo. Bn returned to Cairo on 5 December
	Oct 13	2 RWF arrived at Tidworth from Biebrich, Wiesbaden
1930	Apr 19	HRH The Prince of Wales, as Colonel-in-Chief SWB, visited 1 SWB at the Citadel, Cairo
	Jun 25	John Philip Sousa's march *The Royal Welch Fusiliers* presented to the RWF
	Oct 25	1 SWB embarked aboard transport *Lancashire* at Suez for Hong Kong stopping at Bombay, Colombo and Singapore en route. Arrived 19 November
	Dec 11	1 RWF sailed from India for Sudan. Arrived 19 December. Detachment to Cyprus
1931	Feb 18	2 WELCH moved to Roberts Barracks, Rawalpindi aboard transport *Neuralia* from Singapore. Arrived 1 March
	Oct 9	2 RWF sailed from Southampton for Gibraltar. Arrived 13 October
	Oct 20	1 WELCH moved to Salamanca Barracks, Aldershot from Gosport
1932	Apr 7	1 RWF sailed from Sudan for home. Arrived 21 April and moved to Bhurtpore Barracks, Tidworth
	Apr 16	1 RWF and 2 RWF met at Gibraltar
	Nov 3	2 SWB moved to Catterick Camp from Portsmouth
1933	Mar 28	Presentation of new Colours to 1 SWB by HE Sir William Peel, Governor, at the Race Course, Hong Kong

1934	Apr 1	1/24th Colours (1866–1933) laid up in Brecon Cathedral
	Jul 7–14	2 SWB personnel take part in Northern Command Tattoo at Ravensworth Castle when they re-enact the defence of Rorke's Drift
	Oct 21	2 RWF sailed from Gibraltar for Hong Kong. Arrived 21 November
	Nov 29	1 SWB embarked at Hong Kong aboard transport *Somersetshire* for Karachi. Arrived 15 December
	Dec 10	2 WELCH moved to Landi Kotal, North West Frontier
	Dec 17	1 SWB took over Roberts Barracks, Rawalpindi from 2 WELCH
1935	Sep 12	1 SWB moved to Victoria Barracks, Rawalpindi
	Sep 19	2 SWB embarked at Southampton aboard transport *Somersetshire* for Malta. Arrived at St George's and St Andrew's Barracks, Malta 28 September
	Oct 12	1 SWB took over Roberts Barracks, West Ridge, Rawalpindi
	Nov 12	1 WELCH moved to Victoria Barracks, Belfast from Salamanca Barracks, Aldershot. Sailed from Heysham aboard SS *Duke of York*. Arrived November 13
	Nov 15	1 RWF arrived at Inkerman Barracks, Woking from Tidworth
1936	Mar 25	2 WELCH moved to Akbar Barracks, Agra from Landi Kotal
	Jul 14	2 SWB embarked for Haifa aboard transport *Neuralia* on active service
	Dec 11	2 SWB embarked for Liverpool aboard SS *California* at Haifa
	Dec 21	2 SWB embarked for Londonderry aboard SS *Lairdsmoor* at Liverpool
1937	Jan 3	Regimental Memorial unveiled in memory of the 35 soldiers of the 24th killed in action at Jhelum during Indian Mutiny, 3 July 1857
	Feb 22	1 SWB proceeded to Waziristan in connection with disturbances on the frontier
	Aug 17	2 RWF arrived in Shanghai during the Sino-Japanese war. Remained until 2 February 1938
	Oct 25	1 RWF arrived at Dettingen Barracks, Blackdown from Woking
	Dec 10	1 SWB returned to Rawalpindi following operations in Waziristan
1938	Feb 12	2 RWF sailed from Hong Kong for Sudan. Arrived 3 March
	Mar 1	Presentation of new Colours by HE Marquess of Linlithgow, Viceroy and Governor General of India to 2 WELCH at Agra
	Oct 23	1 SWB moved by train to Landi Kotal from Rawalpindi
	Nov 26	2 RWF sailed from Port Sudan for Bombay. Arrived 5 December and

		moved to Lucknow
1939	Mar 28	2 SWB celebrated 250th anniversary of the raising of the regiment at Londonderry. The Duke of Abercorn, Governor of Northern Ireland was present at Ebrington Barracks
	Apr 13	1 WELCH embarked for Haifa from Belfast, via Heysham and Southampton; hence aboard transport *Somersetshire*. Arrived 3 May
	Sep 3	Start of Second World War
	Nov 13	1 SWB moved to Cawnpore from Landi Kotal

During the Second World War, the Royal Welch Fusiliers had thirteen battalions, six of which served overseas (periods in theatre shown in brackets):

1st	France and Belgium (1940), India and Burma (1942–5)
2nd	India (1939–40), Madagascar (1942), India and Burma (1943–5)
4th	North-west Europe (1944–5)
6th	North-west Europe (1944–5)
7th	North-west Europe (1944–5)
10th	Converted to 6th (RWF) Bn, Parachute Regiment (Aug 1942): North Africa (1943), Greece (1944–5) and Palestine (1945–6)

During the Second World War, the South Wales Borderers and the Monmouthshire Regiment had nine battalions, five of which served overseas (periods in theatre shown in brackets):

1st	Iraq (1941), North Africa (1941–2)
2nd	Norway (1940), North-west Europe (1944–5) – landed on D-Day
6th	Burma, Sumatra (1943–6)
2nd Mons	North-west Europe (1944–5) with 53rd (Welsh) Division
3rd Mons	North-west Europe (1944–5)

During the Second World War, the Welch Regiment had 10 battalions, 4 of which served overseas (periods in theatre shown in brackets):

1st	Crete (1941), North Africa (1942–3), Italy (1943–4)
2nd	Burma (1943–45)
4th	North-west Europe (1944–5) with 53rd (Welsh) Division
1/5th	North-west Europe (1944–5) with 53rd (Welsh) Division

1944	Apr 17	WELCH received the freedom of the City of Cardiff Guard of Honour provided by 5 Infantry Depot and 21 Infantry Training Centre
1945	Oct 22	1 SWB deployed to Haifa in Palestine
1946	Mar	1 RWF re-formed at Wrexham
	Apr 3	2 RWF landed in Japan as part of BCOF from India
	Apr 11	Freedom of Caernarfon conferred on 6 RWF
	Apr 18	1 SWB moved to Cyprus from Haifa. Arrived 25 May
	May 12	6 RWF represented the British Army on the Paris Victory Parade
	Jun	2 SWB moved to Solingen from Erwitte
	Jun 15	Freedom of Wrexham conferred on the RWF
		1 WELCH moved to Opicina Barracks, Trieste from Sirmione
	Jul 16	1 RWF arrived Gevelsberg, Ruhr, BAOR having absorbed men of 4 RWF and 6 RWF
	Aug	2 SWB moved to Harding Barracks, Wuppertal from Solingen
	Dec 9–10	2 SWB moved to Woodfarm Camp, Malvern from Wuppertal
	Dec 27	2 WELCH (1938) Colours destroyed by fire at Kalaw
1947	Feb (mid)	1 WELCH moved to Cavalry Barracks, Udine
	Feb 21	2 RWF sailed from Japan. Arrived Singapore 3 March. To Malaya
	Apr 16	2 SWB lapsed into suspended animation
	Apr 21	2 WELCH moved to Rangoon
	May 23	SWB and MONMOUTHS exercised newly granted Freedom of the County Borough of Newport
	Jun 20	1 RWF moved to Llanelly Barracks, Hubbelrath, Düsseldorf
	Jul 20	Inscription to the Fallen of the Second World War unveiled at the Welch Regiment Cenotaph, Cardiff
	Oct 5	2 WELCH embarked from Burma aboard transport *Lancashire* for Liverpool. Arrived 1 November after an absence from UK of 20 years
	Oct 6	SWB and MONMOUTHS exercised newly granted Freedom of the Borough of Brecon
	Oct	1 WELCH moved to Woodfarm Camp, Malvern with 2 WELCH

1948	Feb 3	1 WELCH moved to Dering Lines, Brecon from Malvern
	Mar 20	2 RWF arrived at Liverpool from Singapore
	Apr 21	2 WELCH disbanded
	May 31	2 RWF reduced to cadre of one officer and three soldiers; then disbanded. 2 SWB disbanded
	Sep 17	Presentation of new Colours to 1 WELCH at Dering Lines
	Oct 9	Bn HQ 4 RWF to Hightown Barracks, Wrexham from Poyser Street
1949	Mar 13	1 SWB moved to Khartoum from Cyprus. Arrived 25 March
	Apr 5	First National Servicemen joined 1 RWF
	Apr 12–8	1 RWF flew to Berlin (Wavell Barracks, Spandau) as part of Berlin Airlift
1950	Jan 4	1 SWB moved to Eritrea from Khartoum
	Mar 22	1 RWF moved from Berlin to Spey Barracks, Buxtehude, Hamburg
	Oct 11	1 WELCH moved to Sobraon Barracks, Colchester
1951	Jan 22	1 RWF arrived at The Dale, Chester from BAOR
	Feb 21	Colours of 2 RWF, 3 RWF and 6 RWF deposited at Caernarfon Castle
	Mar 4	1 RWF departed Southampton on transport *Dilwara* for West Indies
	Mar 27	1 RWF disembarked at Kingston, Jamaica. Companies detached to Newcastle (Jamaica), and British Honduras (Belize)
	May 6	1 RWF detachment to Grenada on Internal Security (IS) duties to end of year
	Jun 14	1 RWF detachment to Antigua on IS duties to July
	Oct 9	1 WELCH embarked aboard transport *Empire Fowey* at Southampton for Korea as part of 29th Infantry Brigade; included 5 officers and 100 men from RWF and 1 officer and 30 men from SWB
1952	Jan 3	RWF Depot Wrexham reopened to train recruits
	Apr 3	2 RWF re-formed at Tidworth
	Sep 16	1 SWB moved to Sennybridge from Eritrea
	Nov 6	1 WELCH embarked at Pusan, Korea aboard transport *Devonshire* for Hong Kong, arrived 13 November
1953	Jan 15	1 SWB moved to Charles Barracks, Brunswick, Germany from Sennybridge
	May 4	2 RWF to Worcester Barracks, Lüneburg, BAOR from Tidworth
	Jun 2	HM The Queen assumed the appointment of Colonel-in-Chief RWF
	July 7	HM The Queen makes Coronation visit to the Borough of Newport. 2nd Monmouths provided the Guard of Honour at Newport Railway Station

	Oct 4	1 RWF to British Guiana on IS duties to end October
	Nov 25–7	HM the Queen's visit to Jamaica
	Nov 28	1 RWF provided Guards of Honour for Sir Winston Churchill KG, President Eisenhower and M Laniel in Bermuda until 12 December
1954	Mar 20	1 RWF arrived at Liverpool from West Indies. To Chisledon Camp, Swindon
	Jun 2	2 RWF from BAOR to Ogbourne St George, Wiltshire
	Jul 23	HM The Queen presented new Colours to 1 RWF, 2 RWF and 4 RWF at Wroughton, Swindon
	Jul 29	1 RWF (1880–1954) Colours laid up in St David's Cathedral (removed to Regimental Museum 1989/90)
	Aug 11	2 RWF sailed from Southampton for Korea on transport *Empire Fowey*
	Aug 15	1 RWF arrived at Moore Barracks, Dortmund from Chisledon
	Aug 26	2 RWF destination changed from Korea to Singapore
	Sep 3	2 RWF disembarked at Singapore and moved to Malaya
	Oct 18	1 WELCH arrived at Southampton aboard transport *Asturias* from Hong Kong. Moved to Llanion Barracks, Pembroke Dock, 16 November
	Nov 30	RWF Alliance with 4th Bn Royal Malay Regt officially approved
1955	Jul 20	1 SWB moved to Dering Lines, Brecon from Charles Barracks, Brunswick for preparation for deployment to Malaya
	Sep	1 SWB embarked on SS *Dilwara* for Malaya
	Oct 15	1 SWB deployed during Malayan emergency
1956	Jun 6	1 WELCH moved to Worcester Barracks, Lüneburg, BAOR via Harwich aboard MV *Vienna* from Pembroke Dock
	Jul 1	6/7 RWF (TA) formed with Headquarters at Caernarfon
	Aug 4	1 RWF moved from Dortmund to Montgomery Barracks, Berlin
	Sep 22	Dedication of new chapel for Welch Regiment at Llandaff Cathedral
	Oct 1	16th (Welsh) Bn Parachute Regiment (TA) re-designated as 6th (Glamorgan) Welch Regiment (TA)
1957	Aug 7	2 RWF disembarked at Southampton from Singapore. To Lichfield
	Sep	1 WELCH moved to Norton Camp, Worcester from Lüneburg
	Sep 28	Laying up of 1 WELCH (1910–48), 2 WELCH (1899–1938) and 3 WELCH (Militia) Colours in Llandaff Cathedral
	Oct 31	1 WELCH moved via Southampton aboard transport *Dilwara* to Aberdeen Camp, Xeros near Lefka, Cyprus

	Dec 31	2 RWF placed in suspended animation
1958	Jan 26	1 RWF arrived at Lichfield from Berlin
	Apr 19	RWF received Freedom of Conwy
	Apr 29	1 RWF sailed from Liverpool on transport *Devonshire* for Cyprus. Arrived 11 May
	May	1 SWB returned to Dering Lines, Brecon from Malaya
	Jul 25	Presentation of new Colours to 1 SWB and 2nd Monmouths by HRH The Duke of Edinburgh at Ebbw Vale, Monmouthshire
	Sep 14	Laying up of 1 SWB (1933–58), 2 SWB (1880–1947), and 3 SWB (1881–1920) Colours in Brecon Cathedral
	Dec 5	1 WELCH moved to Wavell Barracks, Benghazi via Tobruk aboard transport *Empire Fowey* from Alexander Barracks, Dhekelia, Cyprus
1959	Mar 1	Laying up of 2nd Monmouths (1909–58) Colours in St Cadoc's Church, Trevethin, Pontypool
	Jun 24	1 SWB moved to Minden, BAOR from Brecon. Arrived 26 June
	Dec 17	1 RWF disembarked at Southampton from Cyprus. To Carter Barracks, Bulford
1960	Mar 31	Regimental Depots for recruit training at Wrexham (RWF), Brecon (SWB) and Cardiff (WELCH) closed
	Apr 1	Welsh Brigade Depot formed at Cwrt-y-Gollen, Crickhowell
	Apr 8	New Welsh Brigade cap badge adopted. Regimental Headquarters RWF, SWB and WELCH established at Wrexham, Brecon and Cardiff respectively
	Aug 6	Presentation of Colours by HM The Queen at Bute Park, Cardiff to 4 WELCH, 5 WELCH and 6 WELCH (TA)
	Jun 2	RWF Regimental Museum opened at Caernarfon Castle
	Oct 14	1 WELCH departed Benghazi, via Tobruk aboard transport *Dunera* for Southampton. Arrived Maindy Barracks Cardiff 29 October
	Nov 29	Last National Servicemen joined 1 RWF
	Dec 4	Laying up of 5 WELCH (1909–60) in St Catherine's Church, Pontypridd
1961	Feb 26	Laying up of 6 WELCH (1909–60) and 16 PARA (1953–60) Colours in Llandaff Cathedral
	Mar 9	1 WELCH embarked from Alexandra Docks Cardiff aboard transport *Empire Parkston* for the Hook of Holland and Brooke Barracks Berlin
1962	Oct 26	HM The Queen opened Spencer Steel Works at Llanwern. 2nd

		Monmouths provided the Guard of Honour at Newport Railway Station
	Nov	1 SWB moved to Norton Barracks, Worcester from Germany
	Dec 12	1 RWF moved to Singapore for Brunei crisis until February 1963
1963	May 9	1 RWF moved to Aldershot Barracks, Iserlohn, BAOR from Bulford
	May 10	The Welsh Brigade Depot, Cwrt-y-Gollen formally opened by HM The Queen, accompanied by HRH The Duke of Edinburgh. All Welsh Brigade colonels and commanding officers were in attendance
	Jun	1 SWB to Hong Kong (3 platoons deployed on operations in Borneo between 13 February 1965 and March 1966)
	Oct 23–25	1 WELCH moved by air to Rhosse, Cardiff from Berlin and then to Airfield Camp, Netheravon as Infantry Demonstration Battalion
1964	Mar 1	1 WELCH moved to Knook Camp near Warminster
	Jul 14	1 RWF to St George's Barracks, Minden from Iserlohn
	Sep 6	1/24th Colours (1812–25) laid up in Brecon Cathedral
1965	Jul 3	1 WELCH moved to newly completed Battlesbury Barracks, Warminster from Kook Camp
1966	Apr 24	1 RWF to Cyprus as part of UNFICYP until November
	May 31	RWF Alliance with 3rd Battalion The Frontier Force Regiment (Pakistan) officially approved
	Jun	1 SWB returned to Lee Metford Camp, Lydd
	Jun 12	1 WELCH arrived at Fort Stanley Hong Kong from Warminster
	Sep 11	Laying up of 3rd Monmouths (1909–47) Colours in Brecon Cathedral
1967	Jan	1 SWB deployed to Aden on anti-terrorist operations (one company detached to Botswana)
	Apr 1	TA reorganization. 4 RWF, 6/7 RWF, 4 WELCH, 5 WELCH, 6 WELCH and 2nd Monmouths Battalions reduced. WELSH VOLUNTEERS formed
	Apr 7	1 RWF moved to Heathfield Camp, Honiton from Minden
	Sep	1 SWB returned to Lee Metford Camp, Lydd
	Dec 4	Sgt JH Matchett 1 WELCH awarded George Medal for actions whilst commanding a patrol on Hong Kong/China border
1968	June 26	1 WELCH left Hong Kong for Milton Barracks, Gravesend
	Sep 10	Regimental Headquarters RWF moved to The Barracks, Caernarfon from Wrexham

1969	Feb 10	1 WELCH engaged on Public Duties in London
	Mar 14	WELCH celebrated 250th anniversary with a service and parade at the Royal Hospital Chelsea in presence of Field-Marshal Sir Gerald Templer
	Jun 11	1 RRW formed from 1 SWB and 1 WELCH. First Colours presented by HRH The Prince of Wales, as Colonel-in-Chief RRW at Cardiff Castle. RRW exercised newly granted the Freedom of the City of Cardiff
	Jul 1	Investiture of HRH The Prince of Wales at Caernarfon Castle
	Jul 6	1 RRW given the freedom of Borough of Brecon. 1 SWB Colours (1933–58) laid up in Brecon Cathedral
	Jul 8	1 RRW given the freedom of County Borough of Newport
	Jul 10	1 RRW given the freedom of Borough of Carmarthen
	Jul 23	1 RWF flew to Hong Kong. To Gun Club Barracks, Kowloon
	Aug	1 RRW moved from Lydd to Northern Ireland. Until mid-September
	Nov	1 RRW moved from Lydd to Quebec Barracks, Osnabrück from Lydd in AFV 432 mechanised role as part of 12 Infantry Brigade
1970	Mar 1	RWF reverted to regimental cap badge not worn since 1960
	Oct 15	1 RRW four-month tour to Belfast, Northern Ireland. Until 17 February 1971
1971	Feb 7–8	Pte D Bennett 1 RRW awarded George Medal for his actions on the Falls Road, Belfast
	Feb 25–7	HRH The Prince of Wales, as Colonel-in-Chief RRW visits 1 RRW in Osnabrück. Prince of Wales's Platoon Competition instituted
	Apr 1	3rd (V) Bn RWF formed from A and D Coys WELSH VOLUNTEERS and cadres of 4 RWF and 6/7 RWF Bns, and Flint and Denbigh Yeomanry. 3 (V) Bn RRW from companies of the WELSH VOLUNTEERS and 4 (V) Bn RRW from cadre of 4 WELCH
1972	Jan	1 RWF returned to UK from Hong Kong
	Mar 9	1 RWF arrived at Ebrington Barracks, Londonderry
	Mar 27	1 RRW four-month tour to Belfast, Northern Ireland (until 27 July). 6 soldiers killed and 25 wounded
1973	Jan	HRH The Prince of Wales, as Colonel-in-Chief RRW visits 1 RRW in Osnabrück
	Sep 1–6	1 RWF moved to Lucknow Barracks, Tidworth from Londonderry

	Sep 22	2nd Monmouths Colours (1958–67) laid up in St Cadoc's Church, Trevethin, Pontypool
	Oct 26	HRH The Prince of Wales visited SWB Museum, Brecon
	Oct 27	HRH The Prince of Wales, visited Welsh Brigade Depot, Cwrt-y-Gollen, presented first Colours to 3 (V) RRW at Cardiff Castle and attended the RRW Regimental Association Dinner in the City Hall, Cardiff
	Nov 7	RWF received Freedom of the City of Cardiff
	Nov 16	HRH The Prince of Wales, as Colonel-in-Chief, attended RRW Officers' Dining Club dinner at the Hyde Park Hotel
	Nov 25	6 WELCH Colours (1960–67) laid up in Llandaff Cathedral
	Nov 27	1 RRW to Palace Barracks in Northern Ireland as 'Belfast Reserve' battalion as part of 39 Infantry Brigade
	Dec 7	HM The Queen visited the 1 RWF at Tidworth
1974	Jan 27	5 WELCH Colours (1960–67) laid up in St Catherine's Church, Pontypridd
	Feb 20	1 RWF (less two coys) to Belize until August
	Jun 11	HRH The Prince of Wales, as Colonel-in-Chief, visited 4 RRW at Annual Camp at Knook Camp, Salisbury Plain
	Jul	Recruits from Devonshire and Dorset Regiment and Gloucestershire Regiment started recruit training at Cwrt-y-Gollen
	Aug	HRH The Prince of Wales, as Colonel in Chief, attended the RRW Regimental Association Dinner at Dering Lines, Brecon
	Oct 17–27	1 RWF on Operation Spearhead tour to Belfast
1975	Feb 27	1 RWF to Belfast for four-month tour to July
	Sep 1–30	1 RWF on Public Duties, London
	Nov 5	RWF received Freedom of Borough of Arfon at Caernarfon
	Nov 7	HM The Queen presented new Colours to 1 RWF and 3 (V) RWF at Caernarfon Castle
	Dec	Cwrt-y-Gollen renamed as Depot, Prince of Wales's Division
1975	May	1 RRW moved to Brooke Barracks, Berlin
	Jul 27	HRH The Prince of Wales, as Colonel in Chief, visited 3 RRW at Jurby camp, Isle of Man
	Jul 29	HRH The Prince of Wales, as Colonel in Chief, received the freedom of Borough of Llanelli on behalf of RRW

	Nov 2	RRW adopted new cap badge to replace Welsh Brigade badge in use since 1960
	Nov 9–11	HRH The Prince of Wales, as Colonel in Chief, visited 1 RRW in Brooke Barracks, Berlin
1976	Apr 24	RWF received Freedom of Delyn at Mold
	May 6	1 RWF Colours (1954–75) laid up in St David's Church, Cwrt-y-Gollen (removed to St Giles's, Wrexham in 1986)
	Oct 19	1 RWF to Belfast until February 1977
1977	Apr	1 RWF to Ireland for three weeks for Ulster loyalists' strike
	May 7	3 (V) RRW received the freedom of the Borough of Taff-Ely (Pontypridd)
	May 13	1 RRW moved to Normandy Barracks, Aldershot from Berlin
	Jun 24	1 RRW Guard of Honour for HM The Queen's Jubilee visit to Cardiff
	Jul 1	HRH The Prince of Wales, Colonel in Chief, visited 1 RRW at Aldershot
	Aug	1 RRW left Aldershot for a six-month unaccompanied tour to Belize. Based in Airport Camp
	Sep 24	HRH The Prince of Wales presents Colours to 4 (V) RRW at Parc Howard, Llanelli and attended RRW Association Dinner in City Hall Cardiff. 4 WELCH (1960–67) Colours moved to Regimental Museum in Cardiff Castle
	Oct 15	6/7 RWF Colours (1958–67) laid up in Cathedral Church of St Deiniol, Bangor
	Nov 7	1 RWF (based in Manchester) and RRW personnel (South Wales) involved in Op BURBERRY (firemen's strike). Until January 1978
	Dec 2	HM The Queen visited the 1 RWF at Tidworth
1978	Jan 22	1 RWF moved to Lemgo, BAOR from Tidworth
	Feb 27	1 RRW won the ARU Challenge Cup Final – UK
	Apr 30	1 RRW moved to Lee Metford Camp, Lydd for training
	May 4	HRH The Prince of Wales opened The Welch Regiment Museum in Cardiff Castle
	June 12	1 RRW trained at Wainwright, Canada on Ex Pond Jump West 2. Until 12 July
	Sep 30	HRH The Prince of Wales, as Colonel in Chief, visited 3 (V) RRW at Annual Camp, Barry Buddon, Scotland
	Nov 6	1 RWF to Londonderry until March 1979
	Nov 29	HRH The Prince of Wales, as Colonel in Chief, visited 1 RRW at

		Stanford during Northern Ireland pre-training
	Dec 29	1 RRW to Armagh, Northern Ireland on 4-months tour
1979	Jan 21	RRW Commemoration Service in Brecon Cathedral for centenary of Anglo-Zulu war
	May 18–27	Colonel of the Regiment and RRW party visited battlefields for Anglo-Zulu war centenary
	Jul 28	RRW Marches through Cardiff, Newport, Llanelli and Carmarthen to commemorate centenary of Anglo-Zulu war
	Aug 2–11	1 RRW re-enacted defence of Rorke's Drift at Cardiff Tattoo
	Dec	1 RRW party deployed on Op AGILA (Rhodesia Monitoring Force). Until March 1980
1980	Sep	1 RRW moved to Hong Kong as an emergency re-enforcement battalion for 3-months. Until 14 December
	Dec 4	HM The Queen visited the 1 RWF at Lemgo
1981	Feb 4–18	1 RRW on Public Duties, London
	Feb 20	RRW exercised the freedom of City of Swansea granted 29 January
	Feb 25	1 RWF to Belfast from Lemgo until July
	May 7	1 RRW deployed as Spearhead Battalion on an emergency tour at Moscow Camp, Belfast, Northern Ireland during the hunger strikes. Until June
	Jul 29	1 RRW part of Tri-Service Guard of Honour at St Paul's Cathedral for wedding of HRH The Prince of Wales. Battalion also provided street liners in Fleet Street
1982	Jun 11	HRH The Prince of Wales, as Colonel in Chief, visited 1 RRW at Aldershot
	Jun	Adult recruits' training moved from Cwrt-y-Gollen to Whittington Barracks, Lichfield
	Aug 3	1 RWF moved to Battlesbury Barracks, Warminster from Lemgo and Netheravon as Infantry Demonstration Battalion
	Aug 6	1 RRW relieved 1 RWF at Stornoway Barracks, Lemgo. Until 24 June 1988
	Dec 1	Regimental Headquarters RWF moved to Wrexham from Caernarfon
1983	Mar 23	HRH The Princess Margaret visited Welch Regiment Museum
	Sep 17	RWF received Freedom of Borough of Wrexham Maelor at Wrexham
	Sep 19	1 RRW to West Belfast, Northern Ireland. Until 4 February 1984

1984	Jan 4	160 (Wales) Brigade reformed at Brecon
	May 4	HM The Queen visited the 1 RWF at Warminster
	Jul 11–12	HRH The Prince of Wales, as Colonel in Chief, visited 1 RRW at Lemgo
	Oct–Nov	1 RWF moved to Clive Barracks, Tern Hill, Shropshire from Warminster
1985	Feb 21	1 RWF moved to Falkland Islands (air to Ascension then SS Uganda) until June
	Apr 1	Extra rifle company authorised for 3 (V) RWF, 3 (V) RRW and 4 (V) RRW. In addition HSF (Home Service Force) companies raised in each battalion. (HSF Companies disbanded on 31 March 1992)
	Jun 1	HRH The Prince of Wales, as Colonel in Chief RRW, accepted the freedom of Borough of Dinefwr (Llandeilo / Llandovery) at Llandovery and visited 3 RRW and 4 (V) RRW training at Sennybridge
1986	28 Jun	1 RWF to Northern Ireland on Op CARA CARA (Londonderry, Tyrone and Fermanagh) until 21 September
	Sep 20	1 RRW relieved 1 RWF on Op CARA CARA as Incremental Reinforcement Battalion to Northern Ireland. Until January 1987
	Oct 17	Depot at Cwrt-y-Gollen closed
1987	Feb 9	King Goodwill of the Zulus visited Brecon
	Mar 12	HRH The Prince of Wales, as Colonel in Chief, visited 1 RRW at Lemgo
	May	1 RWF to Ballykinler, Northern Ireland
	Jul 11	38th (Welsh) Division Dragon Memorial unveiled at Mametz Wood
	Dec	Headquarters 4 (V) RRW moved to Morfa, Swansea from Llanelli
1989	Jan 1	RRW Brereton History published
	Mar 6	RWF Tercentenary history, That Astonishing Infantry, published
	Mar 16	RWF Tercentenary of formation of the Regiment. Celebrations at Ludlow
	Apr 1	RRW Freedom march at Brecon
	Apr 8	RRW Freedom march at Llanelli
	Apr 21	RWF Tercentenary parade and pageant before HM The Queen, Colonel-in-Chief RWF, at Powis Castle
	Apr 22	Commemorative church service and dedication of relocated RWF Regimental Chapel in St Giles's Church, Wrexham. 3 (V) RRW Freedom march at Taff-Ely (Pontypridd)
	Apr 26	RWF Tercentenary parade, and march through Cardiff

	Jun 23	RRW Officers and Ladies Tercentenary Dinner at the Connaught Rooms attended by HRH The Prince of Wales
	Jun 24	Band & Drums 1 RRW performed at the Royal Hospital Chelsea
	Jul	1 RWF moved to Montgomery Barracks, Berlin from Ballykinler
	Jul 1	RRW Freedom march through Dinefwr at Llandeilo
	Jul 8	RRW Freedom march at Swansea
	Jul 15	RRW Freedom march at Newport
	Jul 19	RRW Freedom march at Carmarthen
	Jul 22	RRW Freedom granted the Freedom of Borough of Brecknock when new Colour Belts were presented by the Borough
	Jul 29	HRH The Prince of Wales, as Colonel in Chief, attended RRW Tercentenary Parade – Cardiff Castle. New Colours presented to 1 RRW, followed by march through Cardiff
	Sep 2	RWF received Freedom of Aberconwy ceremony at Llandudno
	Sep 15	1 RRW awarded Liberty of Warminster
	Nov 12	RRW Tercentenary Service at St Nicholas Church, Pluckley, Kent
	Nov 17	RWF Tercentenary regimental dinner at Brooks' Club, St James's, London
	Nov 18	1 RRW Colours (1969–89) laid up in Llandaff Cathedral
1990	Apr 20	RRW granted the freedom of the Borough of Cynon Valley
	Aug	1 RRW to Stanley Fort, Hong Kong as part of 48 Gurkha Infantry Brigade. Until January 1993
1991	Jun–Jul	RWF 'Save the Regiment' campaign, following Options for Change defence review
1992	mid Aug	1 RWF moved to Mooltan Barracks, Tidworth from Berlin, then (October) Bhurtpore, Barracks, Tidworth
	Nov 7	HRH The Prince of Wales visited 1 RRW in Hong Kong
1993	Jan 11	1 RRW moved to Clive Barracks, Tern Hill, Shropshire from Hong Kong
	Apr 18	RRW granted freedom of the Borough of Neath
	May 13–16	1 RWF to Northern Ireland as Fermanagh roulement battalion. Until November
	Jul 6	RRW Company group to Falkland Islands and South Georgia on 4-months tour
	Oct 1	3 (V) RRW and 4 (V) RRW merged to form 2 (V) RRW

1994	Mar 1	RWF received City of Swansea freedom ceremony
	Apr 15	RWF received Borough of Merthyr Tydfil freedom ceremony
	Jun 5	2 SWB D-Day memorial unveiled at Asnelles, Normandy
	Jun 10	RRW Parade to commemorate 25 years of the appointment of HRH The Prince of Wales as Colonel-in-Chief at Cardiff Castle. 3 (V) RRW Colours re-designated for use by 2 (V) RRW
	Jul 29	1 RWF Regimental Band disbanded
	Aug 6	1 RRW Regimental Band disbanded
	Sep	1 RWF moved to Brawdy, Pembrokeshire from Tidworth
	Sep 2	1 RRW moved to Shackleton Barracks, Ballykelly, Northern Ireland
1995	Feb	1 RWF, less rear party, moved from Brawdy to Bosnia on operational tour until August
	Mar 16	RWF Alliance with the Pretoria Regiment of South Africa officially reinstated
	May 27	4 (V) RRW Colours (1977–93) laid up in Llanelli Parish Church
	Dec	1 RWF moved to Beachley Barracks, Chepstow from Brawdy
1996	Feb	1 RWF, Op FRESCO, fire fighting on Merseyside. Until March
	Mar 23	RRW received the Freedom of County Borough of Merthyr Tydfil
	May 22	1 RWF Colours presentation by HM the Queen at Chepstow
	Jun	HRH The Prince of Wales, as Colonel-in-Chief RRW, visited 1 RRW in Ballykelly and unveiled a Welsh Stone memorial
	Jun 13	Alliance between RRW (previously with The Welch Regiment) and 4th Battalion, The Baluch Regiment officially reinstated
	Aug	1 RRW moved to Cavalry Barracks, Hounslow for Public Duties
	Dec 12	1 RWF moved from Chepstow to Northern Ireland on a six-month operational tour as East Tyrone battalion
1997	Jan 27	RRW Affiliation Parade with 121 South African Infantry Battalion at Mtubatuba, KwaZulu Natal
	Mar 24	2 RWF Boxer rebellion plaque returned to Peking
	May 30	Counties of Glamorgan Army Cadet Force renamed 3 (Cadet) Battalion RRW
	Jun 14	1 RWF returned to Chepstow from Northern Ireland
	Nov 11	1 RWF 1939–40 memorial dedicated at St Venant, Pas-de-Calais
1998	Feb	1 RRW moved to Paderborn, Germany
	Feb	1 RRW to Barker Barracks, Paderborn as part 20 Armoured Brigade

	Apr 1	Friends of the RRW Museums launched
	Jul 8	RWF Carmarthen Right of Entry (freedom) ceremony
	Jun	1 RRW deployed to East Tyrone, Northern Ireland on 6-months tour. Until December 1998
	Jul 17	4 RWF, 6 RWF and 7 RWF Normandy Memorial dedication at Evrecy
	Jul 24	HRH The Prince of Wales visited 2 RRW at Maindy Barracks, Cardiff
	Jul 26	Korean War Memorial to 1 WELCH unveiled in Llandaff Cathedral
	Aug	RWF personnel exchange with the Royal 22ème Régiment of Canada ended
	Aug 17–22	1 RWF moved to Shackleton Barracks, Ballykelly from Chepstow
	Dec	1 RRW returned to Paderborn from Northern Ireland tour
1999	Jan 16–25	1 RRW party with Prince of Wales's Division (Clive) Band to KwaZulu Natal for 120th anniversary of Anglo-Zulu War. Exercise Dead Moon
	May 15	3 (V) RWF final ceremonial parade, Wrexham
	Jul 1	3 (V) RWF amalgamated with 2 (V) RRW to form The Royal Welsh Regiment (RWR)
	Jul 31	RWF Museum reopened after redevelopment
	Oct	1 RRW deployed to Bosnia on Op PALATINE. 1 Platoon to Kosovo with 2 RGJ on Op AGRICOLA. Until April 2000
	Nov 9–10	RWF Memorial unveiled on Ameland, Holland to those lost on the transport *de Valk* in November 1799
2000	Apr 13	1 RWF won Army Rugby Cup
	Jun 27	1/23rd Colours (1826–49) removed from St Peter's Church, Carmarthen for conservation in RWF Museum
	Jul 22	HRH Prince of Wales formally re-opened RWF Museum at Caernarfon Castle
	Aug	1 RWF infantry cricket champions
	Aug 29	1 RWF moved to Clive Barracks, Tern Hill, Shropshire from Ballykelly
2001	May 26	Hornbeam tree planted in Delville Wood, Longueval, France in memory of the 10 RWF's two VCs
	Jun 5	HRH The Prince of Wales visited 1 RRW in Paderborn
	Sep 15	RWF granted freedom of the Borough of Newport
	Sep/Nov	*Regimental Records of RWF* – Volumes VI and VII published

	Nov 1	1 RRW deployed to Pristina, Kosovo as Op AGRICOLA VII. Until May 2002
2002	May	1 RRW returned to Paderborn
	Jun 9	1 RWF (1975–1996) Colours laid up in St Peter's Church, Carmarthen
	Jun 29	RRW granted Freedom of County Borough of Rhondda Cynon Taff at Pontypridd
	Jul–Aug	1 RWF moved to Normandy Barracks, Aldershot from Tern Hill
	Oct	1 RRW deployed on Op FRESCO (firemen's strike) in West Midlands. Until 31 March 2003
	Dec	1 RWF moved to New Mons Barracks, Aldershot
2003	Jun 2	50th Anniversary of HM The Queen becoming Colonel-in-Chief RWF
	Jun 4	HM The Queen and HRH The Duke of Edinburgh visit Regimental Headquarters RWF, Hightown Barracks, Wrexham. Tree planted by Colonel-in-Chief
	Jun 5	Presentation of Colours to RWR by HRH The Prince of Wales in Cardiff Castle
	Oct 4	RRW granted the Freedom of the County of Powys
	Oct 20	1 RRW deployed on Op TELIC 3 in Basra, Iraq as part of Basra City Battlegroup
2004	Feb 20	HRH The Prince of Wales, as Colonel-in-Chief, visits 1 RRW in Basra, Iraq
	Apr	1 RRW returned to Paderborn from Op TELIC 3. 1 RWF to Basra, Iraq on Op TELIC 4. Until October
	May 5	1 RRW returned to Paderborn from Op TELIC 3
	Jun 24	HRH The Prince of Wales, accompanied by Mrs Parker-Bowles, attended RRW Officers' Dinner at Armoury House, London to commemorate the Tercentenary of the battle of Blenheim
	Jul 21	Letter from Chief of the General Staff published promulgating a reduction of four battalions from the future regular army infantry establishment
	Aug	RWF Officers' Association visit to Bavaria for 300th anniversary of the Battle of Blenheim
	Oct	1 RWF returned to Aldershot from Iraq
	Dec 16	Future infantry structure announced: 1 RWF and 1 RRW to become 1st and 2nd Battalions of The Royal Welsh. The Royal Welsh

		Regiment TA to be re-designed 3 R WELSH
2005	Feb	1 RRW moved to Lucknow Barracks, Tidworth from Paderborn
	Apr	1 RRW to Basra on Op TELIC 6
	Sep	1 RWF to Northern Ireland as South Armagh battalion to January 2006
	Oct	1 RRW returned to Tidworth from Iraq
	Nov 29	HRH The Prince of Wales accompanied by HRH The Duchess of Cornwall visited 1 RRW at Tidworth to present medals and meet families
2006	Mar 1	Tri-Unit Guard of Honour formed from WELSH GUARDS, 1 R WELSH and 2 R WELSH at the State Opening of the new Welsh Assembly Government Building – the *Senedd* in Cardiff Bay. Formation of The Royal Welsh with march-past, muster and drumhead service. HM The Queen appointed Colonel-in-Chief, The Royal Welsh
	Mar	1 R WELSH to Salamanca Barracks, Episkopi, Cyprus, with one company on a roulement tour (FIRIC) to the Falkland Islands (until April 2006)
	Jul 18	1 R WELSH – Lebanon Refugees support at Limassol Op HIGHBROW
	Jul 24	1 R WELSH, B Company Gp, to Falkland Islands
	Jul 27	2 R WELSH battlegroup deployment to BATUS Canada on Ex MEDMAN 4 (until 22 September)
	Nov 28	1 R WELSH, A Company Gp, to Falkland Islands to replace B Company Gp (until March 2007)
2007	Mar 1	HM The Queen as Colonel-in-Chief visits 2 R WELSH at Tidworth to present leeks
	Apr 24	1 R WELSH HQ plus Echelon, and B Company Gp to Afghanistan on Op HERRICK (until 16 September 2007)
	May 2	2 R WELSH to Basra on Op TELIC 10 as part of Divisional Reserve Battlegroup. B Company attached to 4 RIFLES Battlegroup (until September). Returned November 2007
	May 7	1 R WELSH, D Company, to Iraq on Op TELIC 10 (until September 2007)
	Oct 19	1 R WELSH, A Company Gp, to Afghanistan on Op HERRICK (until November 2007)
	Nov 1	First edition of the Regimental Journal of The Royal Welsh *Y Cymro* published

	Nov 26	1 R WELSH, D Company Gp, to Afghanistan on Op HERRICK
	Dec 11	2 R WELSH welcome home march through Cardiff and service and medals parade at Millennium Stadium
2008	Jan 15	1 R WELSH A Company Gp to Afghanistan on Op HERRICK (until April 2008)
	Feb 28	HE Prince Mangosuthu Buthelezi presented leeks to 2 R WELSH at Tidworth
	Mar	2 R WELSH public duties at Cardiff Castle
	Apr 12	1 R WELSH B Company Gp to Afghanistan on Op HERRICK
	Jun 5	1 R WELSH medals parade Cyprus on completion of OP HERRICK
	Jun 7	Freedom of the County of Powys exercised by 2 R WELSH at Welshpool
	Jul 28	1 R WELSH moved to The Dale Barracks, Chester from Cyprus
	Aug 30	Freedom of Bridgend County Borough exercised by 2 R WELSH
	Sep 5	Freedom of Wrexham County Borough exercised by 1 R WELSH
	Sep 13	Freedom of the City and County of Swansea exercised by 1 R WELSH
	Nov 7	Memorial plaque to Sir Tasker Watkins VC unveiled in Welch Regiment Chapel, Llandaff Cathedral
	Nov 11	1 R WELSH Christmas Truce Memorial, Frelinghiem, France unveiled
2009	Feb 21	Freedom of the Vale of Glamorgan Council exercised by 2 R WELSH at Barry
	Feb 28	3 R WELSH adopted new cap badge
	Feb	2 R WELSH C Company deployed to Afghanistan, Op HERRICK 10
	Mar 9	1 R WELSH & 2 R WELSH adopted new cap badge
	Mar 28	Freedom of Neath Port Talbot County Borough Council exercised by 2 R WELSH at Neath
	Apr 24	Freedom of Flintshire County Council exercised by 1 R WELSH at Mold
	Apr 25	Freedom of Gwynedd Council (formerly Arfon District) exercised by 1 R WELSH at Caernarfon. Freedom of Ceredigion County Council exercised by 2 R WELSH at Aberystwyth
	Aug	2 R WELSH A Company deployed to Afghanistan, Op HERRICK 10
	Aug 22	2 R WELSH C Company medal parade Cardiff Castle. Mrs Danielle Harkett, widow of LCpl C Harkett presented with Elizabeth Cross
	Sep 5	1 R WELSH parade through Wrexham

	Sep 9	Freedom of County of Carmarthenshire granted and exercised by 1 R WELSH at Carmarthen.
	Dec 15	1 R WELSH main body deployed to Afghanistan, Op HERRICK 11 as part of Op MOSHTARAK. Returned 4 May 2010
2010	Mar 27	Freedom of County Borough of Rhondda Cynon Taf exercised by 2 R WELSH at Ynysangharad Park, Pontypridd
	Apr 27	HM The Queen accompanied by HRH The Duke of Edinburgh visit The Royal Welch Fusiliers Museum at Caernarfon Castle.
	May 1	Home Coming and Freedom parade A Company, 2 R WELSH at Brecon. Elizabeth Crosses presented to the mothers of Pte R Hunt and Pte J Prosser.
	May 29	Home Coming and Freedom parade B Company, 2 R WELSH at Newport.
	Jun 5	Home Coming Parade and granting of the freedom of West Chester and the City of Chester, exercised by 1 R WELSH. Granting of the Freedom of County Borough of Torfaen at Pontypool; exercised by A Company, 2 R WELSH.
	Jun 10	HM The Queen, as Colonel-in-Chief R WELSH, attends Medal Parade and Regimental Garden Party at Chester Racecourse. Regimental Association of The Royal Welsh launched.
	Jun 26	Firing Line: Cardiff Castle Museum of the Welsh Soldier officially opened by HRH The Prince of Wales. National Armed Forces Day parade Cardiff.
	Jul	B Company 2 R WELSH deploy to Afghanistan
	Sep 18	Granting of the Freedom of Conwy County Borough to 1 R WELSH at Llandudno
	Sep 25	Granting of the Freedom of Caerphilly County Borough exercised by 1 R WELSH at Caerphilly and Blackwood.
2011	Feb 19	Granting of the Freedom of Blaenau Gwent County Borough exercised by 2 R WELSH at Ebbw Vale
	Feb 24	B Company, 2 R WELSH return from Afghanistan
	Mar 4	Granting of the Freedom of Monmouthshire County Borough exercised by 2 R WELSH at Monmouth
	Apr 7	Reaffirmation of the Freedom of Merthyr Tydfil County Borough exercised by 2 R WELSH at Merthyr Tydfil

Apr 30	Homecoming parade of 2 R WELSH at Cardiff
Jun 11	Granting of the Freedom of Denbighshire County Borough exercised by 1 R WELSH at Denbigh
Jul 23	Granting of the Freedom of the City of Bangor exercised by 1 R WELSH
Nov 5	St David's Chapel, Llandaff Cathedral dedicated as The Royal Welsh Memorial Chapel